Edward D. Cope

On the Batrachia and Reptilia of Costa Rica

With notes on the herpetology and ichthyology of Nicaragua and Peru -

Vol. 1

Edward D. Cope

On the Batrachia and Reptilia of Costa Rica
With notes on the herpetology and ichthyology of Nicaragua and Peru - Vol. 1

ISBN/EAN: 9783337383053

Printed in Europe, USA, Canada, Australia, Japan

Cover: Foto ©Andreas Hilbeck / pixelio.de

More available books at **www.hansebooks.com**

ON THE

BATRACHIA AND REPTILIA

OF COSTA RICA.

WITH NOTES ON THE

HERPETOLOGY AND ICHTHYOLOGY OF NICARAGUA AND PERU.

BY E. D. COPE.

Art. IV.—*On the Batrachia and Reptilia of Costa Rica.*

By E. D. Cope.

Costa Rica, the most southern of the states of Central America, lies between eight and eleven degrees of north latitude, and presents great inequalities of surface. Its length is traversed from northwest to southeast by the range of the Cordilleras, which rise in their highest point, the Pico Blanco, in the southern part of the republic, to an elevation of 11,800 feet. In the middle of the country the range forms the western border of a plateau whose elevation is about 5000 feet, and whose eastern rim is marked by a chain of volcanoes. The principal rivers of the country, which flow into both oceans, take their rise in this plateau. Here also the more important part of the population dwells. in the two towns of San José and Cartago.

The climates of the eastern and western regions present material differences. The eastern slope of the country receives the trade-winds loaded with the moisture and clouds derived from the evaporation of the Caribbean Sea under a tropical sun. Constant rain falls on the mountain sides, and the rivers flowing into the Caribbean Sea are remarkable for the volume of water they contain as compared with the length of their courses. The climate of the country west of the mountains is much drier, but not so much so as to constitute aridity. The entire republic, but especially the eastern region, is covered with a dense tropical vegetation.

Dr. Wm. M. Gabb, from whose explorations much of my information is derived, has discovered that the major part of the rocks of the country are of miocene age, and that the elevation of the Cordilleras took place after the close of that period of geologic time. The volcanoes bounding the plateau on the east are of later age.

The material on which the present investigations are based consists chiefly of two collections. One made by Dr. Van Patten of San José was derived from the country in the neighborhood of that city. The larger collection, made by Dr. Wm. M. Gabb of Philadelphia, under the auspices of the government of Costa Rica, was obtained in the southern portion of the region of Costa Rica which lies east of the elevated mountain range which traverses that country, and at different elevations on the range itself. According to Mr. Gabb, the most elevated point, the Pico Blanco, in the southern part of the State, rises to the height of 11,800 feet above the sea. The coast region includes a wide belt of swamps, and then gradually rises to a height of two hundred feet at fifteen miles inland. From this point the surface rises rapidly, so that at twenty-five miles the elevation is 2500 feet above the sea. The vegetation of the entire region is exceedingly dense. At an elevation of from 5000 to 7000 feet is the region of greatest precipitation ; rain falls here, according to Mr. Gabb, on more than two hundred days of the year, and heavy fogs are of daily occurrence. The surface is often covered with a deep layer of moss, and swamps abound. There is no belt of pines, as in Mexico, but the extreme summits of the peaks are covered with a sparse vegetation consisting chiefly of an *Artemisia* much like that of the Rocky Mountain region of the United States, with whortleberries, a bamboo-like grass, a stunted tree fern, and scattered tufts of grass.

The collections were made at Limon and Old Harbor, on the coast, and from the latter locality inland to the foot of the Pico Blanco, and thence to its summit. The principal inland stations were Sipurio, fifteen miles from the coast, elevated 200 feet, and Uren, twenty-five miles, elevated 2500 feet. Opportunity being thus offered for determining their hypsometrical distribution, I give the following lists of species which occur at different elevations. Thus certain species do not occur further inland than ten miles from the coast ; these are : *Dendrobates typographus ; D. tinctorius auratus ; D. talamancæ. Bufo auritus* is a coast species. From Sipurio we have nearly all the snakes and lizards, and the following Batrachia : *Hyla gabbii, H. uranochroa,* and *H. elæochroa ; Bufo hæmatiticus.* From between this point and Old Harbor came *Mocoa assata* and *Opheobatrachus vermicularis.* From Uren, *Cranopsis fastidiosus* and *Trypheropsis chrysoprasinus.* From higher points on the Pico Blanco, chiefly in the rainy zone, at from 5000 to 7000 feet, we have the following list :—

BATRACHIA.

Opheobatrachus vermicularis, Gray,
Œdipus morio, Cope.
Crepidius epioticus, Cope.
Ollotis cœrulescens, Cope.
Atelopus varius, Stann.
Hyla nigripes, Cope.
Hyla punctariola, Peters.
Phyllobates hylæformis, Cope.
Lithodytes podiciferus, Cope.
Lithodytes muricinus, Cope.

Lithodytes habenatus, Cope.
Lithodytes melanostictus, Cope.
Lithodytes megacephalus, Cope.
Lithodytes gulosus, Cope.
Hylodes cerasinus, Cope.
Ranula brevipalmata, Cope.

OPHIDIA.

Catostoma psepholum, Cope.
Contia calligaster, Cope.
Bothriechis nigroviridis, Peters.

Sixteen species of *Batrachia,* three of *Ophidia,* and none of the other orders. On the summit of the Pico Blanco Mr. Gabb obtained the *Gerrhonotus fulvus* of Bocourt, the only lizard obtained from above the base of the mountains, and the extreme southern point of distribution of the genus *Gerrhonotus*, so far as yet known. It is worthy of remark that the elevated regions between 2500 and 7000 feet are the habitat of four genera with rudimentary auditory apparatus, while but one (*Atelopus*) presenting that character was discovered by Mr. Gabb in the lower country. Three of the four genera of frogs with imperfect organs of hearing known from South America, viz.: *Alsodes*, *Phrynobatrachus*, and *Telmatobius*, are also from mountainous regions.

The Aguacate Mountains to the west of the plateau furnished a species of lizard to the collection, the *Chalcidolepis metallicus*.

The collection obtained by Mr. Gabb embraces eighty-nine species, viz.: *Testudinata*, 5; *Lacertilia*, 19; *Ophidia*, 35; and *Batrachia*, 30. The number of species not previously known to science is thirty-seven. A report on a collection made by Dr. Van Patten in the valley of central Costa Rica was published by the writer in the Proceedings of the Philadelphia Academy for 1871, p. 204, which included forty-six species. Of these twenty-six do not occur in Mr. Gabb's collection. The names of these species are as follows:—

BATRACHIA.

Agalychnis moreletii, Dum.
Smilisca baudinii, Dum. Bibr.

LACERTILIA.

Phyllodactylus.
Cyclura acanthura, Wiegm.
Sceloporus malachiticus, Cope.
Anolis hoffmannii, Peters.
Anolis nannodes, Cope.
Anolis insignis, Cope.
Anolis microtus, Cope.

`OPHIDIA.

Epicrates cenchria, L.
Colobognathus dolichocephalus, Cope.
Colobognathus brachycephalus, Cope.
Colobognathus hoffmannii, Peters.
Colobognathus nasalis, Cope.

Colosteus rhodogaster, Cope.
Ninia atrata, Hallow.
Ninia sebæ, D. B.; *maculata*, Pet.
Tantilla melanocephala, L.
Rhadinæa serperaster, Cope.
Conophis lineatus, Dum. Bibr.
Liophis epinephelus, Cope.
Herpetodryas carinatus, L.
Drymobius margaritiferus, Schl.
Dipsas gemmistratus, Cope.
Thrasops mexicanus, D. B.
Dryiophis brevirostris, Cope.
Pelamis bicolor, Daud.
Elaps multifasciatus, Jan.
Elaps ornatissimus, Jan.
Elaps nigrocinctus, Gird.
Bothriechis affinis, Boc.
Crotalus durissus, L.

A number of species, chiefly batrachians, have been sent to the Smithsonian Institution by C. N. Riotte, which are of considerable interest. In addition to the collections sent to the United States, others have been sent to Europe, and have been the objects of study by M. Bocourt of Paris, Peters of Berlin, Günther of London, and Keferstein of Göttingen. The explorers who have furnished the material to these herpetologists have been Messrs. Hoffmann, Salvin, and Seebach. The total number of species known from the investigations, now amounts to one hundred and thirty-two. But many species have been described from the adjoining states of Nicaragua and Chiriqui, and from Veragua, adjoining the latter, of which many will be found to enter Costa Rica also. Thus it is evident that this region is very rich in terrestrial cold-blooded vertebrata. The State of Costa Rica is about equal in extent to that of South Carolina.

BATRACHIA.

GYMNOPHIONA.

1. SIPHONOPS MEXICANUS, Dum. Bibr., viii. 284.

From the forest country near the coast at Limon.

URODELA.

2. OPHEOBATRACHUS VERMICULARIS, Gray, Ann. Mag. Nat. Hist. 1868, 297. *Œdipina uniformis*, Keferstein, Archiv. für Naturgesch., 1868, 299.

Three specimens, one from the Pico Blanco, at 6000 feet elevation, of large size, measuring m. .162 in length. The cranium of this one is completely ossified above, but the choanæ are not isolated, but open into the orbit by a wide fissure. The two other specimens are from the lower country, twenty miles from the coast.

3. ŒDIPUS MORIO? Cope, Proc. Academy Philadelphia, 1869, p. 103.

A partly preserved specimen from the eastern slope of the Pico Blanco.

ANURA.

BUFONIFORMIA.

4. CRANOPSIS FASTIDIOSUS, Cope, gen. et sp. nov. Bufonidarum.

Char. Gen.—No ostia-pharyngea nor tympanum; no vomerine teeth. Cranial integument entirely occupied by a rugose ossification; parotoid glands present. Fingers and toes distinct, the latter palmate.

This genus is *Peltaphryne*, Cope, with the auditory apparatus wanting. *Char. spec.*—Size of the *Bufo lentiginosus*. The head wide, not depressed, the cranial ridges consisting of elevated canthus rostralis, supra- and post-orbital border and a supra-tympanic crest extending to the parotoid gland. These, especially the last, are obtusely thickened. The supra-tympanic crest is produced downwards behind the orbit as a rugose osseous plate to opposite the inferior border of the pupil of the eye, bounding the position usually occupied by the membranum tympani by a rough concave margin. The canthus rostrales are short and inclose a groove between them; the loreal and labial regions are rugose with small tubercles. The profile of the muzzle descends abruptly to the lip, which it does not overhang. The nostrils are as far removed from each other as each one is from the orbit. The posterior outline of the cranial ossification is squarely truncate in adults.

The parotoid glands are short, subtriangular, sublateral, and as deep as long. They are not continued into a fold. The upper surfaces of the body and limbs are studded with round warts, so closely on the latter region as to resemble a pustular disease. A row of larger tubercles extends from the parotoid gland to the axilla. The inferior surfaces support numerous smaller tubercles. The fingers are short and free, and the palmar tubercles are very obtuse. There are neither tarsal folds nor tubercles, those of the sole being very obscure. Toes half-webbed. The end of the longest toe reaches the end of the muzzle when the limb is extended, and the longest finger reaches the vent.

The color above is yellowish-brown; below, dirty brown. A blackish band extends from the parotoid to the axilla, the color not affecting the apices of the tubercles in its course, and sometimes extending to the abdomen. Throat with a black spot; top of head yellow or brownish-yellow.

		M.
Length of head and body .	.	.058
" to orbit	.	.005
" to posterior border of cranium	.	.016
" to axilla . .		.023
" of fore limb	.	.035
" of hand	.	.013
" of hind limb .	. .	.060
" of hind foot	. .	.035

Several specimens from 2500 feet elevation on the slope of the Pico Blanco, in the district of Uren.

5. CREPIDIUS EPIOTICUS, Cope, gen. et sp. nov. *Bufonidarum*.

Char. Gen.—No ostia-pharyngea, membranum tympani, nor vomerine teeth; parotoid gland present. Cephalic derm not occupied by ossification. The digits of all the feet inclosed in the skin, leaving the longest median toe projecting; inner digits of both feet rudimental.

In this new genus the structure is much as in *Atelopus*, resembling also, but in

25

less degree, the genus Oedipus of the salamanders.   In other respects the form is that of *Ollotis*, Cope.

Char. Specif.—Size medium ; cranial crests consisting of supra-tympanic, supra-orbital, and canthal ridges, the last two continuous with each other and extending in a nearly straight line to the nares, with a slight thickening opposite the front of the orbit. The intervening concave surface is of moderate width. The superciliary ridges send inwards a short tuberosity at the posterior third of the orbit. The supra-tympanic is short and very protuberant, giving the cranium an angulate outline. There is a low, narrow, post-orbital ridge. No trace of membranum tympani. Parietal region with several small osseous nodules on each side. Parotoid very small, subround. Skin everywhere rugose with minute tubercles, which are sparse on the dorsal, dense on the ventral, regions. Soles smooth, no tarsal, carpal, or solar tubercles or folds. Longest digit on both extremities projecting 2.5 phalanges beyond the flat mass which includes the other digits. Femur half-inclosed in inguinal integument. A concave dermal fold from end of each sacral diapophysis to parotoid gland, which is easily obscured.

		M.
Length of head and body	.	.035
" to orbit . .		.004
" to angle of jaw	.	.011
" to axilla	.	.017
" to groin		.030
" of fore limb	.	.019
" of fore foot . . .	.	.007
" of hind limb (free portion)	.	.030
" of hind foot	.	.018

General color black, above a little lighter with a few darker spots on each side ; soles yellowish ; entire scapular region brown ; sometimes a brown median dorsal band.

From 5000 feet elevation on Pico Blanco.

6. OLLOTIS CŒRULESCENS, Cope, gen. et sp. nov. *Bufonidarum.*

No ostia-pharyngea nor membranum tympani. Parotoid glands present. Digits free on all the feet.   Cranial derm not occupied by ossification.

This genus may be regarded as *Bufo* with the auditory apparatus incomplete, agreeing in this respect with the preceding genera *Crepidius* and *Cranopsis*.

Char. Specif.—The largest specimen is about an inch in length, and hence perhaps not adult, although there are no marks of immaturity observable. There are no cranial ridges except a protuberant supra-tympanic ; the superciliary ridges are slightly prominent and continued behind in straight lines by two angles of the parietal bone. No trace of membranum tympani. The canthus rostrales are straight and angular, and the lores elevated ; the nares are nearer to each other than each is to the orbit. The tongue is large and elongate. The skin of the back and sides is studded with numerous spaced tubercles, and the lower surfaces are nearly smooth. There is no tarsal fold, and the palmar and plantar tubercles are obsolete. The digits are all distinct, those of the hind foot half-webbed. The wrist of the fore limb, and the end of the second toe of the hind limb extended, reach the end of the muzzle.

		M.
Length of head and body	.	.025
Width of head behind	.	.008
Length to orbit . .	.	.003
" to axilla	.	.010
" to groin .		.021
" of fore limb	.	.014
" of fore foot	.	.005
" of hind limb . .	.	.023
" of hind foot		.013

Upper surfaces blackish, the tubercles brown ; below black, thickly marked with light blue spots.

From 3000 to 5000 feet elevation on Pico Blanco.

7. BUFO AURITUS, Cope, sp. nov.

Vertex flat, bounded by a vertical superciliary crest on each side, which is slightly bent where it gives off the postorbital crest, and then continues to the posterior border of the cranium. Post-orbital ridge prominent, presenting an open angle where it gives off the supratympanic, particularly prominent as the anterior border of the tympanic membrane. Supratympanic horizontal, prominent. Supraorbital crests abruptly incurved at the loreal region, and separated by a narrow groove at the summit of the muzzle. No preorbital crest. End of muzzle narrow, produced beyond the line of the upper lip ; external nares nearer each other than the orbit. Parotoid gland quite small, surmounted by several dermal spines. Tubercles of the skin small, spinulose, most numerous on the sides, wanting below. Tarsus without fold, spinulose ; palmar and solar tubercles insignificant. Digits elongate, the fingers remarkably so ; the toes half-webbed. The wrist reaches beyond the end of the nose, as does also the heel of the extended hind limb. The membranum tympani is distinct in its anterior half, and the ostia-pharyngea are minute.

				M.
Length of head and body	.	.	.	.031
Width of head behind	.	.	.	.010
Length to orbit .	.	.	. .	.004
" to posterior border skull .			. .	.010
" to axilla	.		. .	.015
" to groin	.	.	. .	.026
" of fore limb	.	.	.	.023
" of fore foot	.	.	.	.010
" of hind limb	.	.	.	.038
" of hind foot	.	.	.	.021

Color brown; a quadrate patch on vertex from orbits to occiput, an oblique band from the latter outwards on each side, and a spot on each lateral sacral region black. Belly marbled with black; throat and limbs below, dusky.

This species resembles in its general appearance the *Crepidius epioticus*, Cope, but differs in many points, both generic and specific. It is also allied to the *Bufo veraguensis*, Schmidt, but according to that author the supra-tympanic crest is much smaller than in *B. auritus*.

Two specimens from the East coast region.

8. BUFO VALLICEPS, Wiegm. *B. nebulifer*, Girard, U. S. Mex. Boundary Survey, II. (2) 25, Pl. XL. f. 1.

A variety with narrow cranial crests, and less fully webbed toes; the ground color is light, and is marked with large black spots forming a row on each side of the median line. Throat and breast black, pale spotted.

BUFO COCCIFER, Cope. Proceed. Acad. Philada., 1866, p. 130.

Parotoids round semi-globular. Muzzle narrowly rounded, nearly as long as orbit. Strong bony, canthal, pre-, sub-, and postorbital, supratympanic and supraorbital ridges; the last regularly curved and sending a parietal branch towards the median line; the first rapidly converging, leaving only a gutter between. Tympanum one-fifth orbit. Everywhere minutely tubercular, those of the sides and forearm conic; soles rough, web short, metatarsal tubercles small, obtusely prominent; tarsal fold scarcely visible. Heel to axilla. Two obtuse metacarpal warts.

Gray brown; a yellow vertebral line, with numerous chestnut brown light bordered spots on each side. Sides with two longitudinal brown bands; one from parotoid and one from groin. Limbs irregularly light varied above. Under surface immaculate.

Length of head and body 2 in. 6 l.; breadth at angle of jaws below, 1 in.; length of fore limb 1 in. 5 l.; length of foot 1 in. 3 l.

C. N. Riotte. Smithsonian collection, No. 6490.

This handsome species resembles the *B. ocellatus*, Gthr., in coloration.

10. BUFO STERNOSIGNATUS, Günther, Catal. Batrach. Salientia Brit. Mus. 1858, p. 68.

Said to have been found in Costa Rica by Keferstein, Archiv. für Naturgeschichte, 1868, 294.

11. BUFO AGUA, Daudin.

Large and small specimens from the Eastern coast. This species is especially abundant about houses.

12. BUFO HÆMATITICUS,* Cope, Proceed. Acad. Philadelphia, 1862, 157. Sipurio.

FIRMISTERNIA.

13. HYPOPACHUS VARIOLOSUS, Cope. *Engystoma variolosum*, Cope, Proceed. Acad. Philada. 1866, p. 131; Proceed. Amer. Philos. Soc. 1869, p. 166. *Hypopachus seebachii*, Keferstein, Nachrichten Göttingen, 1867, p. 352; Archiv. f. Naturgeschichte, 1868, Tab. IX., figs. 1, 2.

The genus *Hypopachus* resembles *Engystoma*, but differs in the important particular of the possession of a claviculus, as was first pointed out by Dr. Keferstein. It is therefore to be referred to the family of the *Phryniscidæ*.

Two strong compressed metatarsal tubercles, a sublongitudinal cuneiform and subtransverse opposite it: toes slightly webbed. Width between tympanic regions nearly double the length from muzzle to nuchal fold. Muzzle prominent, as long as orbit, nostrils nearly terminal. Mandible with two symphyseal notches, and median knob. Tongue flat, elongate; slits of vocal vesicle large. Heel to front of scapula.

Dark brown above; under side, limbs, and belly darker, with numerous large yellowish spots. Sides anteriorly blackish-brown, which color has a serrate margin above. Femora, forearms, and tarsi brown behind, with coarse yellow vermiculations: some yellow spots behind the angle of the mouth. Length of head and body 1 in. 4.5 l.; of posterior limbs 1 in. 7 l.

Chas. N. Riotte. Mus. Smithsonian, No. 6486.

---

* The *Bufo simus*, Schmidt, Denkschriften K. K. Akademie Wien, 1858, p. 254, will probably be found in Costa Rica.

26

14. ATELOPUS VARIUS, Stannius.

Very abundant both on the Pico Blanco range, and in the lower country. The markings are vermilion on a black, or, in the case of the mountain specimens, a green ground. In some of the latter the red markings are few, and in others altogether wanting, leaving a uniform pea-green.

15. DENDROBATES TYPOGRAPHUS, Keferstein, Archiv. f. Naturgeschichte, 1868, p. 298, Pl. IX. fig. 7.

Dendrobates ignitus, Cope, Proceed. Academy, Phila., 1874, p. 68.

The form described by me as D. ignitus differs from the one observed by Keferstein, in the uniform red of the dorsal region. Both occur in Mr. Gabb's collection.

From the low country, not more than ten miles inland.

16. DENDROBATES TINCTORIUS, Wagl., var. auratus, Girard, Steindachner Verhandl. der K. K. Zool. bot. Gesselsch., Wien, 1864, p. 261.

Numerous, and exclusively from the lower country, not extending far inland.

17. DENDROBATES TALAMANCÆ, Cope.

Allied to the Dendrobates lugubris, Schmidt, Denkschr. K. K. Akad., Wien, 1858, p. 250.

First finger longer than the second; the skin of the upper surfaces entirely smooth; tympanic membrane very obscure. Head elongate, muzzle depressed, truncate, the nares equidistant from each other and the orbits. When the limbs are extended, the wrist reaches the front, and the heel the middle of the orbit. No tarsal fold; palmar and solar tubercles insignificant.

Color brown above, separated by a border of light pigment from the white of the lower surfaces. This border continues as a light border of the upper lip round the end of the muzzle. Top of muzzle, and a band from the eye to the groin on each side, yellowish. Upper surface of fore limbs yellow. External surfaces of femur and tibia covered with a light pigment. Posterior face of femur black, with a short yellow band on each side directed outwards from behind the groin, forming with the light band of the superior face of the femur, a hook-shaped pattern.

	M.
Length of head and body .	.022
" of head to angle jaw	.008
Width of head behind .	.006
Length to orbit .	.003
" to axilla	.010
" of fore limb .	.011
" of fore foot .	.005
" of hind limb .	.027
" of hind foot .	.012

From near Old Harbor on the East coast.

ARCIFERA.

18. HYLA GABBII, Cope, sp. nov.

A rather large species resembling the *Smilisca baudinii*, D. B. Vomerine teeth in two short transverse series between the interior nares. Choanæ and ostia pharyngea subequal; tongue round, scarcely free behind. Head short, wide; canthus decided, concave; nares much nearer each other than each one is to the orbit. Membranum tympani less than half the area of the orbit. Integument of upper surfaces nearly smooth. Fingers well webbed to the base of the penultimate phalange of the longest; toes webbed to near the end of the corresponding phalange of the hind foot. Digital dilatations large, about equal to the tympanum. Lower surfaces areolate.

Color ashy-brown, the pigment forming a narrow band on the upper face of the femur. Anterior and posterior faces of femur dusky, without coloration figure. Some large irregular brown spots on the back, groin marbled with light-brown and white. Lip with a faint pale border, no large spots on it or the lores. Tibia and cubitus with broad pale-brown cross-bands; lower surfaces all whitish.

		M.
Length of head and body		.056
" of head to angle of jaws		.016
Width of head at angle of jaws		.020
Length to orbit		.007
" to axilla		.022
" of fore limb		.032
" of hind limb		.093
" of hind foot		.040

This tree-frog resembles the *Smilisca baudinii*, but differs in the absence of the post-orbital process, the more extensive palmation of the fingers, and the absence of the characteristic spots on the upper lip. It is dedicated to William M. Gabb, of the Geological Survey of Costa Rica (formerly of Santo Domingo and of California), to whom herpetological science is indebted for the collection now described.

From near Sipurio.

19. HYLA URANOCHROA, Cope, sp. nov.

A species of the size of the *Hyla carolinensis*, and related to it in general structure. The vomerine teeth are in two fascicles exactly between the inner nares, which are small and just equal to the ostia pharyngea in size. Tongue round, little free. The head is wide and the muzzle rounded, the canthus rostralis obtuse and moderately concave. Nostrils considerably nearer each other than to orbit, which is large and equal to twice the area of the tympanum. The toes are short, and digital dilatations large; the fingers have a short web, which is deeply emarginate; the toes are not fully webbed, the membrane notched to opposite the proximal end of the antepenultimate phalange. Head and body elongate, so that when the limbs are closed the knee and elbow are not in contact. The heel reaches the middle of the orbit, and the longest finger the femur. Skin smooth above, areolate below.

Color above, blue; below ? yellow (whitish pigment in alcohol). The blue pigment is sharply bordered along the sides and extends on the upper surfaces of the humerus and femur, as well as cubitus, tibia, and tarsus, and on the base of the outer finger, and entire surface of outer two toes. Upper lip yellow bordered all round; vent yellow, no inguinal, femoral, labial, or other spots.

			M.
Length of head and body	.		.040
" to angle of jaw	.		.010
" to axilla	.	.	.014
" to groin	.	.	.036
Width of head behind	.		.014
Length of fore limb	.		.022
" of fore foot	.	.	.010
" of hind limb	.	.	.055
" hind foot	.	.	.025

From near Sipurio.

20. Hyla nigripes, Cope, sp. nov.

A species of the size of *Hyla carolinensis*, with longer head and limbs than the last described species. Vomerine teeth in two short transverse series between the inner nares; the latter equal to the ostia pharyngea. Tongue longer than wide. The head is an oval, but the muzzle does not project; the canthus rostrales are a little concave, and the lores are oblique. The orbits are large and from four to five times the area of the tympanum. The digital dilatations are moderate, the web of the fingers extending about half-way to the end of the longest, notched deeper than the line of the penultimate phalange. Web of toes not extending to end of penultimate phalange. Upper surfaces smooth, the lower finely areolate.

Color dark-brown, limbs and feet blackish. Lip brown, groin finely white and blackish marbled; no lateral border or band. Posterior face of femur black, unspotted; no spots on any other region. Sides of throat black-dusted.

		M.
Length of head and body . .		.039
" to orbit		.005
" to angle of jaws . .		.011
Width of head at angle of jaws	.	.013
Length of fore limb . . .	.	.024
" of fore foot . . .	.	.010
" of hind limb . . .	.	.065
" of hind foot . . .	. .	.016

When the limbs are closed, the knee and elbow overlap some distance. The species in form and sombre colors resembles some of the *Scytopes*, but is a true *Hyla*.

13. HYLA ELÆOCHROA, Cope, sp. nov.

A small species with elongate oval head and uniform coloration. The vomerine teeth are entirely between the nares, and form two short series directed backwards towards the middle line; in some specimens the backward inclination is very slight. The choanæ are larger than the ostia pharyngea, and the tongue longer than wide. The muzzle is elongate and plane above, and slightly projecting. The nares are as far from each other as from the lip border, and nearly twice as far from the orbit. Eyes large, four or five times the area of the membranum tympani. Digital dilatations large; fingers entirely free. Toes with emarginate webs not reaching the end of the antepenultimate phalange of the longest toe, which is rather short. Skin above smooth, below finely areolate on the abdomen. Legs long, the heel reaching the end of the muzzle, the wrist not quite reaching the same point.

Color above and below a uniform olivaceous, without spots. A pale area below the eye; lip faintly marbled.

	M.
Length of head and body . .	.026
" to angle of jaws . .	.009
Width of head at angle of jaws .	.009
Length of head to orbit . .	.0045
" to axilla . . .	.011
" of fore limb . . .	.016
" of fore foot . . .	.007
" of hind limb . . .	.044
" of hind foot . . .	.019

27

The pre-frontal bones in this species are unusually wide.

Three specimens from the east foot of the mountains near Sipurio.

19. HYLA PUNCTARIOLA, Peters, Monatsberichte K. Preuss. Acad. Wiss. 1863, p. 462.

Five specimens from the Cordilleras, at from 5000 to 7000 feet, agree in essentials with the above-named species, but differ entirely from it in coloration, as well as from each other. Two of the specimens agree with each other exactly in this respect, and as *Hylæ* are, as far as my experience extends, very constant in coloration, I suspect that the forms below described are true species.

The *H. punctariola* is distinguished by the posterior position of its vomerine teeth, the small tympanic membrane, and the free fingers. In all of the Costa Rican specimens the fingers are not entirely free, but a web extends between the outer two to the middle of the first phalange. The area of the tympanum in the same is one-fourth that of the orbit. The head is short and wide, and the heel extends nearly or quite to the end of the muzzle.

Subspecies *pictipes:* color light brown above, not sharply bordered on the sides, below white. Edge of upper lip, tarsus, and outer toe, white. The sides are marbled with dark-brown and yellow from near axilla to groin; and the front and back of the femora on each side of the superior brown longitudinal band are yellowish-brown, spotted with bright yellow. Two outer toes brown, inner toes yellow. Humerus, cubitus, and two outer fingers, brown above. Back, lips, and belly, unspotted. Two specimens.

Subspecies *mœsta.* Above brownish-black, sides and femora, except above and below, deep black. Some white spots on sides behind axillæ, and some small yellow ones near groin. A few minute white points on front and back of femur, and upper surfaces of feet. Otherwise the limbs and hands, except the thumb, are black. Lower surfaces thickly black spotted except on breast and tibia, where the white predominates. One specimen.

Subspecies *monticola.* Color light grayish-brown with large dark-brown spots, forming transverse bars, one between the eyes, one in front of the scapulæ, one behind the scapulæ, and one at the sacrum. Below unspotted white. Limbs with light-brown surfaces above; concealed surfaces pale, unspotted. No inguinal spots; a few specks of brown on sides. Length of head and body .037 m. Size of H. p. *mœsta* identical; of H. p. *pictipes* a little smaller. One specimen.

The original *H. punctariola* is from Veragua, Panama.

Before leaving the genus *Hyla*, I may mention that the *Hyla polytænia*, Cope, (Proc. Amer. Philos. Soc. 1869, p. 164) has been described by Prof. Peters as *H. striata* (Monatsber. K. Preuss. Acad. 1872, p. 681).

20. SMILISCA BAUDINII, Dum. Bibr. (*Hyla*).   *Smilisca*, Cope.

San José, Dr. Van Patten.

21. AGALYCHNIS MORELETII, A. Dum. (*Hyla*).   *Agalychnis*, Cope.   *Hyla holochlora*, Salvin.

San José, Dr. Van Patten.

22. PHYLLOBATES HYLÆFORMIS, Cope, sp. nov.

A species of medium size, resembling a *Hyla* in its habit. The head is a broad oval, and the muzzle is not produced, but is depressed. Interorbital space wide, plane; canthus rostralis obtuse, straight, lores oblique. Tongue an elongate oval narrowed before, flat, and one-half free. Ostia pharyngea very minute; membranum tympani one-sixth of orbit. Fingers and toes free, dilatations rather large. Skin smooth above and below.

Color above rich brown, divided on the vertebral line by a narrow red stripe. Femora light brown before and behind. Gular region with large vocal sac, of a rose color. Abdomen and inferior surfaces of femur and tibia with a rosy or orange pigment.

	M.
Length of head and body	.027
" to orbit	.003
" to angle of jaws	.009
Width between angle of jaws	.010
" orbits	.003
Length fore limb	.017
" fore foot	.006
" hind limb	.037
" hind foot	.018

From the mountain of Pico Blanco, at 7000 feet elevation.

23. LIYLA GUENTHERII, Keferstein, Archiv für Naturgeschichte, 1868, p. 296.

Allied to the species of *Lithodytes*, and unknown to me.

24. LITHODYTES PODICIFERUS, Cope, sp. nov.

Allied to the *L. conspicillatus*. The head and body short, and the hinder limbs long. Canthus rostralis straight, end of muzzle truncate, not projecting beyond lip. Vomerine teeth in two short series entirely behind the internal nares, but directed forwards and outwards towards them. Outline of mouth an oval. Muzzle plane above, parietal region slightly concave. Membranum tympani two-thirds the size of the orbit. Ostia pharyngea a little larger than choanæ. Nostrils much nearer to each other than to the orbits. Skin smooth. The muzzle extends beyond the wrist of the appressed fore limb, and marks a point a little beyond the middle of the tibia.   Digital dilatations very small.   All the specimens from the level of from 5000 to 7000 feet.

The colors of this species vary remarkably, more than I have observed to be the case in any other frog.   All of the varieties agree in having a large triangular brown patch below the vent, a dark line along the canthus rostralis, and dark crossbars on the legs.   They differ as follows:—

Var. A. Dark-brown above and below; speckled on the lower surfaces with dirty-white; side of head deep-brown to membranum tympani.   Sometimes a white vertebral line, and a transverse one like it on the posterior face of the femur. Numerous specimens, all from 7000 feet on the Pico Blanco.

Var. B. Similar to the last, but with a bright rufous spot extending from the eye forwards to the lip border; a white spot from the tympanic disc downwards and backwards.   Two specimens.

Var. C. Cherry-red everywhere except on the abdomen; a brown spot below the eye, one behind the tympanum, and several on the back.   Sole of tarsus and foot black.   One specimen.

Var. D. Dirty-white, with four longitudinal brown bands above.   An oblique brown band from orbit to abdomen, ceasing at the middle of the side.   A broad blackish band with pale centre from groin upwards parallel to and well removed from the other oblique band.   Lower surfaces white.   One specimen.

The small digital dilatations and obtuse muzzle are characters which distinguish this frog from the *L. conspicillatus* as at present defined.

25. LITHODYTES MUNICINUS, Cope, spec. nov.

Canthus rostralis straight angular, muzzle narrowly truncate.   Tympanic disc equal eye.   Vomerine teeth in two short transverse fasciculi behind the internal nares, well separated from each other, and not extending outwards beyond the line of the inner border of the inner nares.   Tongue elongate, flat, and extensively free behind.   Digital dilatations small; the heel of the extended hind limb marks the end of the muzzle.

Sides of head and body and upper surfaces of limbs black, unspotted; below light-brown unspotted; above uniform red purple.

		M.
Length head and body .	.	.0200
" to angle of jaws .	.	.0075
" of fore limb .	.	.0110
" of hind foot .	.	.0150

The shorter hind limbs and larger tympanic membrane, with the more transverse and widely separated vomerine teeth, distinguish this from the last species. Represented by one small specimen from the Pico Blanco.

29. LITHODYTES HADENATUS, Cope, sp. nov.

This species, also represented by one specimen, agrees with the *Lithodytes muricinus* in the points just enumerated in which it differs from the *L. podiciferus*. Its general color is blackish-brown above, and dirty-white below. On each side above, a white band extends from the orbit to the middle of the side, where it is continuous with the pale color of the abdomen. The vomerine teeth are in small fasciculi, well separated, and both behind and within the line of the nares.

		M.
Length of head and body .	.	.022
" hind limb . .	.	.037
" hind foot . .	.	.015

From the Pico Blanco.

30. LITHODYTES MELANOSTICTUS, Cope, sp. nov.

A species of distinct type from the preceding in its short head and longer body. Size of *Rana temporaria*. The vomerine teeth are in two short transverse series entirely behind the inner nares, well separated from each other and not extended outwards beyond the line of the inner margin of the nares. Choanæ and ostia pharyngea sub-equal; tongue sub-round, one-third free, and a little emarginate behind. Head flat, wide, muzzle projecting a little, canthus rostrales straight convergent. Nostrils more than twice as far from orbits as from end of muzzle; their distance apart 1.33 times in their distance from the orbit. Loreal region and lip oblique. Diameter of eye equal distance from its border to the nostril, its area four times that of the membranum tympani, which is a rather narrow vertical oval. Skin everywhere smooth. Limbs long, dilatations of fingers large, of toes moderate. The muzzle marks the middle of the cubitus and a little beyond the middle of the tibia. The order of lengths of the fingers is, 1-2-4-3; first and third toes equal. The sternum is a wide cartilaginous shield notched at the end. There is a well-developed zygomatic process of the squamosal bone, but no corresponding malar process.

			M.
Length of head and body . . .	.	.	.050
" to angle of jaws (axial)	.	.	.015
Width of head at angle of jaws .	.	.	.022
Length to orbit (oblique) . . .	.	.	.007

28

Length to axilla .	.	.	. .019
Width of sacrum	.	.	. .009
Length of fore limb .		.	. .037
" of fore foot .		.	. .019
" of hind limb .		.	. .096
" of hind foot .		. .	. .045

Ground-color above, brownish-gray; below, dirty-white. The limbs are cross-banded rather distantly with blackish, the bars extending on the front and back faces of the femur as well as on the upper surfaces. A white median band from muzzle to vent, which is bounded on the sides at different points with blackish. A pink band extends from above each tympanum to the end of the ilium, and is broadly bordered with black on the outer side, this color extending on the sides of the animal as oblique black spots. The tympanum is black and sends a black bar to the rictus oris; two black bars pass directly from the orbit to the lip, and another by the canthus rostralis and nares to the same.

One specimen from 7000 feet elevation on the Pico Blanco.

31. Lithodytes megacephalus, Cope, sp. nov.

A large species with the physiognomy of a *Ceratophrys*. Head very large, wide, and depressed, with oblique lips and lores. The end of the muzzle descends obliquely from the nares to the lip. Orbit as long as the distance from its border to the nostril, which is close to the line of profile, and distant from its fellow two-thirds its distance from the orbit. Canthus rostralis distinct, not prominent, very little concave. Orbits oblique, the superciliary borders rising from the end of their anterior third into a strong ridge, which runs in a straight line and terminates abruptly in a slight thickening at the posterior border of the cranium. The posterior half of the cranium above is thus deeply grooved, while the top of the muzzle is plane. The tympanic membrane is a vertical oval equalling one-third the area of the opened eye; its long diameter enters the latter 1.75 times; its short diameter, three times. The vomerine teeth are in two short approximated series entirely behind the posterior borders of the choanæ. Each is convex forwards, and does not extend exterior to the line of the inner boundary of the choanæ. The tongue is oval, longer than wide, and widest behind where it is entire. Ostia pharyngea larger than choanæ. The limbs are short, and the fingers and toes entirely free. The dilatations are small, especially on the hands, but the terminal phalanges are T-shaped. The wrist extends beyond the end of the muzzle, while the heel only reaches to the middle of the orbit. There is a small but prominent obtuse cuneiform bone at the base of the inner toe; other than this there are no folds or tubercles on the tarsus or carpus.

The skin is smooth on the upper and lower surfaces, with the following exceptions: A dermal fold extends from each exoccipital region on each side of the back, pursuing a concave course to the middle of the transverse process of the sacrum. A similar fold extends from the vent on each side, in an oblique direction to the end of the transverse sacral process. Sides of body areolated.

The exoccipital bone sends inwards and backwards a recurved crest, in anticipation, as it were, of the "parieto-quadrate" arch of *Ceratophrys*. There is also a strong zygomatic process of the squamosal, but no malar process to meet it.

The color above, in spirits, is a light ash; below white, the sides of an intermediate shade. A black spot extends from the tympanum to the scapula, and sends a line to the eye. The posterior face of the femur is black marbled distally with ash; the black extends as a well-defined patch to the vent. Entire sole of foot black. Legs distantly cross-banded above. Lips brown; some small dark spots on the lower rim of the orbit. The breast, abdomen, and lower side of femur and tibia are marked with black, forming a figure like the refuse of the plates of a button-maker, *i. e.*, representing the interstices between large confluent white spots.

		M.
Length of head and body .	. `	.070
" to orbit (oblique) . .	.	.011
" to angle of jaws (axial) .	. .	.025
Width at angle of jaws .	. .	.035
" of interorbital region	. .	.007
" of sacrum . .	. .	.017
Length of fore limb . .	. .	.038
" of fore foot . .	. . .	.016
" of hind limb . . .	. . . .	.092
" of hind foot	.	.045

This species is intermediate between the *Ceratophrydine* group of *Cystignathidæ* and the *Hylodine*, and illustrates the propriety of their union as I proposed in 1865. I find no technical characters by which to separate it from *Lithodytes*, in which genus it is analogous to the *Hylodes sulcatus* in the genus *Hylodes*, where the same elevation of the superciliary borders appears. With present experience in the genus *Bufo*, such a character does not appear to warrant generic separation.

A female specimen, containing eggs ready for deposit, was taken by Mr. Gabb on a spur of the Pico Blanco, at 6000 feet elevation.

32. LITHODYTES GULOSUS, Cope, sp. nov.

The description of the *L. megacephalus* applies in many details to the present frog. Thus, the vomerine teeth, tongue, tympanum, cranial crests, and extremities are the same. The differences are seen in the absence of dermal plicæ, the coloration, and perhaps in the larger size. The color is a dark leather brown, except on the pectoral and abdominal regions and inferior surfaces of the femur and tibia, where the brown is irregularly marbled with white. There is a black spot across the tympanum and one under the eye.

The type specimen is a female containing mature eggs, and is twice as large as the type of the *L. megacephalus*, equalling the *Gnathophysa ocellata* in bulk. Its head is relatively smaller than in that species. Thus the width enters the length of head and body in the former, more than twice; in the latter, less than twice; the length of the head enters the same in the *L. gulosus* three times; in the *L. megacephalus* 2.66 times.

	M.
Length head and body	.103
" head to orbit (oblique)	.015
" head to angle jaws	.030
Width head at angle jaws	.047
" head between orbits	.008
Length fore limb	.060
" fore foot	.022
" hind limb	.138
" hind foot	.065

The sternum of this species is a large cartilaginous plate, wide and deeply emarginate behind, and slightly narrowed in front. From the same locality as the last species.

33. HYLODES CERASINUS, Cope, sp. nov.

A slender species with oval head, and large digital dilatations. The vomerine teeth are in two fasciculi well separated from each other, and well behind the line of the internal nares, at the extremities of two longitudinal ridges, which diverge slightly forward towards the inner margin of the choanæ. The latter are about the size of the ostia pharyngea. The tongue is of a narrow oval form. The head is flat and the lores oblique. The muzzle is not produced beyond the lip, but is narrowed towards the end, the canthus rostralis being concave. The nostrils are twice as far from the orbit as from each other. Orbit large, tympanic membrane distinct, very small, one-eighth the area of the eye. The skin is smooth above in the specimen, which is soft through the effect of weak spirits; skin of sides and abdomen areolate. Limbs rather long, digits long, free. The wrist and heel of the extended limbs reach the end of the muzzle. The lengths of the fingers are in order, commencing with the shortest, 1-2-4-3. Dilatations truncate.

		M.
Length of head and body .	.	.035
" to orbit (oblique)	.	.006
" to angle jaws	.	.013
Width to angle jaws .	.	.013
" between orbits	.	.0032
Length of fore limb .	.	.022
" of fore foot .	.	.009
" of hind limb .	.	.055
" of hind foot	.	.024

The sternum of this species is a parallelogrammic cartilaginous plate, deeply notched distally and not distinguished into style and disk.

General color brown above, white below. A rose-colored vertebral band. Four pale lines from orbit and one from nostril cross the upper lip. Anterior half of sides finely reticulate with black, groin cherry-red. Upper posterior face of femur and inner face of tibia cherry-red; lower posterior face of femur brown punctate with white.

This beautiful species is apparently related to the *H. bicumulus*, Peters, from Venezuela, but differs in several points. In *H. cerasinus* the nares are terminal, many times nearer the end of the muzzle than to the orbit; in *H. bicumulus* less than twice as far from orbit as from snout. The tympanic disk is smaller in the *H. cerasinus*, and the coloration entirely different. These comparisons are rendered possible by the fulness of Prof. Peters's description, and it is a gratification to refer to them as models worthy of imitation in all departments of biology.

One specimen from the eastern slope of the Pico Blanco.

34. GNATHOPHYSA OCELLATA, Linn. (*Rana*); *Cystignathus*, Dum., Bibr.; *Gnathophysa*, Cope.

From the east side of the Cordillera.

RANIFORMIA.

35. TRYPHEROPSIS CHRYSOPRASINUS, Cope, Proc. Acad. Philada., 1868, p. 117. *Ranula*, do., Cope,
l. c. 1866, p. 130.

From Uren, 2500 feet.

In examining a collection sent to the Smithsonian Institution from Costa Rica, from Charles N. Riotte, I was much surprised to notice what was apparently a *Hylorana* near *H. erythræa*. Doubting the correctness of the locality, I laid the frog away. Having since seen other and allied species from Tropical America, I recognize the existence of a genus representing *Hylorana*, but differing in the important particular of the incompleteness of the ethmoid arch, its superior plate being represented by cartilage. In the present species the terminal phalanges are slender, and furnished with a transverse limb, though the dilatations are small; the latter are distinct in the *Rana cæruleopunctata*, Steindachner; in an undescribed species from Vera Paz the transverse limb is very small, but present.

The generic characters then are—

Ethmoid arch superiorly cartilaginous; prefontals narrow, longitudinal, widely separated. Distal phalanges slender, with transverse limb; no metatarsal shovel; tongue bifurcate.

The species is allied to the above named, but has a relatively shorter muzzle and limbs. Nostril nearer end of muzzle than orbit (equidistant in *cæruleopunctata*); muzzle 1 and 1-5th orbit (1 and 2-5ths Steind.). Under jaw anteriorly abruptly truncate. Canthus rostralis straight, strong, muzzle acuminate from its extremity, projecting; loreal region vertical. Tympanum elliptic, two-thirds orbit. Vomerine teeth weak, in convergent fasciculi behind opposite nares. Skin shagreened above, a glandular fold on each side. The longest finger cannot be extended to vent; heel to middle loreal region. Toes fully and widely palmate, three distal phalanges of fourth free; one minute metatarsal tubercle.

Color brilliant leek-green, the groin and belly approaching golden; a golden band from lip to shoulder, and a faint one on each side of back. Limbs above, and tarsus and forearm below, black, the femur with a few golden spots on black ground behind. Head dark above, from eye to shoulder black; below pale yellowish-green, immaculate, except some dark shades on sternal regions.

Length of head and body 1 in. 9 l.; of fore limb 1 in.; of hind limb 2 in. 7.5 l.

36. RANULA BREVIPALMATA, Cope, loc. cit. 1874, p. 131.

The upper lip and lower surfaces brown spotted. From Pico Blanco.

REPTILIA LACERTILIA.

LEPTOGLOSSA.*

37. Mocoa assata, Cope, Proceed. Acad. Phila. 1864, p. 179.

From Old Harbor; originally described from the west coast of Salvador.

38. Mabuia alliacea, sp. nov.

Distinguished by its long acute muzzle, and reduced number of rows of scales. The former exceeds the width of the head between the eyebrows, and is narrow at the end. There are seven superior labial scuta, of which the fifth subtends the orbit, and is very elongate. The internasals are very narrow and are separated above by a small median scutum in front of the internasal. This scale may be abnormally distinct. Interfrontonasal wider than long, in contact with frontal; latter long, narrowed behind, its apex received into a notch between the frontoparietals.

* Epaphelus sumichrastii, Cope, gen. et sp. nov.

Char. Gen.—A scincoid allied to *Gymnophthalmus*, without eyelids. Toes 4–5. Nostril in a single plate; no supranasals; one loral. Frontonasals distinct. One large supraocular, and one large supraorbital; frontoparietals and interparietal confluent; parietals distinct. Scales large, smooth, and subequal. Meatus auditorius open.

This genus is characterized by the greater simplicity of the cephalic scuta than any of the genera of this group with toes 4–5.

Char. Specif.—Twelve rows of scales on the body. Labial scuta 4/4, the last inferior very narrow. Behind the symphyseal is a very large mental, which is a little wider than long, and behind it two pairs of large transverse infralabials meet on the middle line. The frontal is very small, scarcely one-fourth the size of the supraorbital, which is a little larger than the interfrontonasal, and much less than the interparietal. Behind each parietal are two transverse scales, each pair separated on the median line by a scale like those of the back. Three scales margin the vent, of which the median is the least. The extremities appressed to the sides fail to meet by the length of the hand.

Color light rose-color, metallic on the upper surfaces, the tail bright pink, the top of the head bluish. Sides of head and body to groin deep brown, the color abruptly defined above; below unspotted.

												M.
Total length	.	.	.	.	.	.	.	.	.	.	.	.0450
Length to vent	.	.	.	.	.	.	.	.	.	.	.	.0205
" to axilla	.	.	.	.	.	.	.	.	.	.	.	.0090
" to ear	.	.	.	.	.	.	.	.	.	.	.	.0038
" of fore leg	.	.	.	.	.	.	.	.	.	.	.	.0010
" of hind leg	.	.	.	.	.	.	.	.	.	.	.	.0065
" of hind foot	.	.	.	.	.	.	.	.	.	.	.	.0037

Since the above description was written I have obtained a specimen of identical proportions, but of twice the size. It was obtained by Dr. Francis Sumichrast in the western part of the State of Tehuantepec, and is of interest as the first naked-eyed scinc discovered in Mexico. It is dedicated to its discoverer, who has added so largely to our knowledge of that country.

Four supraorbitals, second large. Interparietal longer than wide, separating the wide, undivided parietals. Two transverse narrow occipitals. Nuchal scales equal those of the body, which are in twenty-seven rows. Preanal scales three, large and subequal; subcaudal scales small except where reproduced, when they are transverse and narrow. When the limbs are appressed to the sides the ends of the toes mark the middles of the fingers.

Color above, sap-green shaded with brown, below leek-green. A light blue band from the lip to the groin; a pale shade from the eyebrow to above the femur, brown bordered above. From the low country.

The large preanal scuta and long muzzle distinguish this species from the *M. cepedei*.

39. MABUIA CEPEDEI, Gray; Cope; Proceedings Academy Phila., 1862, p. 186.

With twenty-eight rows of scales. From below Sipurio.

40. CHALCIDOLEPIS METALLICUS, Cope; gen. et spec. nov. Ecpleopidarum.

Char. Gen.—Dorsal scales smooth, in uninterrupted transverse annuli round the body, the size subequal on the various regions, including the nuchal and gular. Toes 5–5, all clawed. Superior head shields; interfrontonasal, two prefrontals, a frontal, two frontoparietals, two parietals separated by an interparietal. Tympanum distinct; nostril in the single nasal plate. No femoral pores. Teeth compressed, with a principal cusp and a denticle on each side.

This genus is one of the *Ecpleopidæ*, but presents a manifest resemblance to the *Chalcididæ* in its squamation. The absence of the lateral band of small scales, and continuity of the transverse series across the median line of the back, distinguish it from certain genera of the family, and the uniform character of the squamation of the neck and body distinguishes it from others.

Char. Specif.—A slender lizard with very long tail and feeble limbs. The head is narrowed and acute in front, with produced rostral shield. The interfrontonasal plate is as wide as long, and the frontal elongate. There are four supraorbitals on each side. The interparietal is elongate and with parallel sutures with the larger parietals. The latter are bounded externally by a large temporal, forming with them a diagonal suture. These are all bounded posteriorly by a series of four shields across the occiput, and these again by a transverse series of seven scales larger than those of the nape which follow them. The nasal plate is followed by a large loreal, and this by a smaller preocular. Seven superior labials; their relative lengths, beginning with the shortest, are, 5–7–6–2–1–3–4. Two pairs of infralabial scuta are in contact on the median gular region, of which the posterior pair are twice as long as the first; there are twenty scales in a cross-row between the angles of the lower jaw. There is some irregularity in the pectoral scales which gives the last row of the neck the appearance of a collar. Twenty-three series of scales in an annulus of the body; twelve transverse rows between the large post-occipital row and the line of the axillæ, and forty-three to the line of the posterior faces of the femora. There are two large longitudinal anal scuta, which embrace a scale between them on the anal border; they are preceded by another large pair, but of reduced size.

The tail is nearly twice the length of the head and body, and the hind limb is one-fourth the latter measurement.

							M.
Total length	.	.					. 0.165
Length of head and body	.						. .058
" to axilla	.	.					.017
" of head to tympanum							.011
" " to orbit	.		.				.0045
" of fore limb	.		.	.			.0130
" of hind limb	.	.	.	.	.	.	. .0145

The limbs are surrounded by large scales except on the concealed faces of the humerus and femur, where the scales are small and flat.

The color is light gray with red and green metallic reflections; the sides are brown, and the middle of the back darker than a line above the brown of the side. Near the light bands a few scales are blackish, forming a row on each side. Below dusted with brown. Head with deep brown sides and white upper lip. Sides of tail brown with a zigzag upper margin.

The lower eyelids of this species are very narrow, and having been dried I cannot ascertain the presence or absence of a transparent disk.

This new lizard was found by Mr. Gabb on the Aguacate Mountains.

41. AMIVA FESTIVA, Licht. and Von M. *A. eutropia*, Cope, Proc. Ac. Phila., Feb. 1862.

In adult males the dorsal band is wanting. The central preanal plate is frequently followed by two scuta but little smaller.

42. AMIVA GADDIANA, Cope, sp. nov.

Abdominal scuta in eight longitudinal series, median gular scuta but little larger than those surrounding them. Premaxillary teeth 4-1-4. Mesoptychial scales in a single row of one median and three rapidly diminishing laterals on each side; the border of the collar with minute scales. One row of brachial scuta nearly continuous with two rows of antebrachials. One principal row of rather

30

small postbrachials. Anal scuta; one large round submedian disk, and two or three much smaller in advance of it. Two rows of large tibial scuta, with a few odd scuta on the inner side. No anal nor heel spurs. Nostril on the naso-internasal suture. Frontal scute rather short, undivided; parietals and interparietals short, followed by a few scales larger than the granular ones which cover the back and the nape. The hind limb extended reaches the front of the tympanum by the end of the longest toe; the fore limb extends to just beyond the end of the muzzle.

		M.
Total length	.	.215
Length to vent	.	.082
" to axilla	.	.035
" to tympanum	. .	.017
" to orbit	. .	.008
Width of head at angle of jaws	. .	.013
Length of hind limb	. . . . .	.056
" of hind foot	. . . .	.030

Color olivaceous; two lateral light bands separated by a darker shade than that of the dorsal interval, and crossed, like the side below the lower line, by black bars. Below immaculate, or with black spots on the gular region.

Three specimens of this species were obtained at Old Harbor by Mr. Gabb, to whom I dedicate it. Its affinities are with the *A. guttata*, Wiegm.

DIPLOGLOSSA.

43. DIPLOGLOSSUS MONOTROPIS, Kuhl.
44. GERRHONOTUS FULVUS, Bocourt, Bulletin Archives du Museum, 1872, p. 104.

Agrees with the description of Bocourt excepting in having the prefontal plates distinct, and in having a narrow dark band on each side of the back.

From the summit of the Pico Blanco.

NYCTISAURA.

45. COLEONYX ELEGANS, Gray, Ann. Mag. Nat. Hist., 1845, p. 162; Dumeril, *Gymnodactylus colconyx*, Archives du Museum, 1856, p. 483; *Brachydactylus mitratus*, Peters, Monatsber. K. Preuss. Akad., 1863, p. 42.

Costa Rica, fide Peters.

46. PHYLLODACTYLUS, indet.

47. SPHÆRODACTYLUS GLAUCUS, Cope, Proceed. Acad. Philada., 1865, p. 192.

Variety with dark bordered interscapular and sacral transverse spots. Near Sipurio.

18. THECADACTYLUS RAPICAUDUS, Houtt.

Mouth of Estrella or North River, E. coast.

IGUANIA.

49. ANOLIS MICROTUS, Cope, Proceedings Academy Philadelphia, 1871, p. 214.

Auricular opening not larger than nares. Scales generally larger than in *A. insignis;* four rows between orbits, two rows of large ones above orbits; seven rows between rows of canthus rostralis at middle of muzzle, three loreal rows at middle; three large smooth infralabial rows. Scales of tail and fore leg three or four keeled.

Brown with cross-bands of large paler ocelli crossing the sides behind the axilla, at middle, and at crura. Eye and a broad band to shoulder, dark brown.

Description.—Scales of back, sides, and belly equal and smooth. Tail compressed at base, distally cylindric, covered with equal scales. Front without ridges but with well-marked concavity; all the scales covering it equal and smooth. Occipital or parietal region concave, with high lateral posterior bounding ridges, which do not unite, but leave a notch between them (in one specimen). Occipital region covered with small scales. Zygomatic arch prominent, canthus rostralis not tubercular. Face well developed. First two infralabial scales larger than the others. Limbs short, stout; anterior not reaching groin; posterior extending to angle of lower jaw. Dilatations well developed.

		M.
Total length	.	. 0.31
Length to orbit		.015
" to ear	. .	.03
" to axilla	. . .	·05
" to groin	. . . . .	.0955
" to convergence of parietal crests	.	.029
" of fore foot	. .	.017
" of tibia	.	.0183
" of hind foot	. . .	.027
Width at anterior angle of orbits		.0125
" at zygomatic arch	. .	. .017

This species is darker than the next, and is much less ornamented. The color is a rich yellowish-brown; where the epidermis is lost on the head a strong yellow pigment appears, so that it is probable that it could in life change to that color at will. A deep brown band commences by covering the whole eye and extends to the shoulder, where it is marked by pale centred ocelli. It is separated above by a narrow paler band from a large dark brown patch that covers the nape and scapular regions. Limbs and tail broadly and indistinctly brown cross-banded. Belly and throat immaculate.

San José, Costa Rica ; Dr. Van Patten.

This large species is allied to the next, but perhaps resembles more the *Anolis biporcatus*, Wiegm., the largest *Anolis* of Mexico. The latter has, among other points of difference, keeled abdominal scales and a shorter muzzle, with very different coloration. The uniform size of all the scales is a noteworthy character of the *A. microtus*.

50. ANOLIS INSIGNIS, Cope, Proceed. Academy Philadelphia, 1871, p. 213.

Auricular opening half as large as eye. Scales intermediate ; seven rows between orbits ; one or two supraorbital rows but little larger than the others ; eight rows across middle of muzzle, and six across loreal region at middle. Three large and two small keeled infralabial rows. Scales of arm smooth, of tail striate.

Fawn-brown, with four double bands of greenish-blue between axilla and tail. Between these the brown is divided by a yellow band which widens below and breaks into spots above. A large round greenish-blue spot with brown centre in front of axilla.

Interorbital and occipital regions deeply concave, the latter bounded posteriorly by two elevated osseous ridges which meet behind at an acute angle. No facial rugæ, front flat except a slight median elevation. Muzzle with broad median ridge. Scales of front equal, those of canthus osseous. Postfrontal and zygomatic arches prominent, rugose. Inferior loreal row of scales larger than others, nares surrounded by small scales. Fan very largely developed. An elevated crest or dermal fold on the nape. Scales of the sides and back (except some median rows) flat, pavement-like, equal, smooth, one-third the size of the smooth ventrals. Four median dorsal rows subconic, smaller than the ventrals. Tail proximally compressed, covered with equal scales. Limbs stout, the anterior extending four-fifths way to groin ; the hinder reaching nearly to the ear. Scales of the limbs small ; dilatations distinct.

The colors of this *Anolis* are very elegant. Besides the large spot behind the angle of the mandible, there is a blue one on the angle surrounded by fawn-color, and this by yellow. Sides of the temporal region and neck with yellow spots. Bluish of first cross-band in a coarse netted figure. Top of head fawn-color ; face entirely vermilion ; belly light yellow. Tail with broad blackish annuli ; limbs with dark cross-bars, three on tibia, femur, and forearm ; two on humerus.

		M.
Total length	. .	. 0.440
Length to orbit	. . .	. .0183
" to ear	. . . .	. .037
" to axilla	. . .	. .062
" to groin	. . .	. .135
" to angle of parietal crests		. .035
Width at anterior angle orbits .		. .014
" at zygomatic arches		. .019
Length of fore foot .	.	. .023
" of tibia	. .	. .029
" of hind foot .	.	. .040

From San José. Dr. Van Patten.

This is a large species, being about equal to the *A. edwardsii* of Jamaica. It is one of the most elegantly colored among the species of a beautiful genus. Its affinities, as already pointed out, are to the *A. squamulatus*, Peters, which is very near the *A. laticeps* of Berthold.

51. ANOLIS COPEI, Bocourt, Mission Scientifique de Mexique, Reptiles, p. 77, Pl. xv., f. 10, 10 a.

Three specimens from Old Harbor. Color in life blue and brown. This animal haunts sunny spots on the edge of the forest.

52. ANOLIS TROCHILUS, Cope, Proceed. Acad. Philadelphia, 1871, 215.

Specimens from Talamanca and San José.

Abdominal scales small, flat, smooth; tail cylindric, with similar scales. Dorsal scales smaller than ventral, pavement-like, very weakly keeled, graduating into those of the lower part of the side, which are smaller. Head moderately elongate; width between anterior margins of orbit equal length of muzzle from same point, measured on the side. Interrugal concavity of the front well marked, occupied by very small scales, much less than those of the rugæ, in nine rows. Scales between rugæ and canthus large. Two rows separate the superciliaries, which are separated by three or four rows from the occipital. Five rows of loreal scales. Six smooth scales in the supraorbital disc, three inner large, transverse, the three outer longitudinal. Four rows of infralabials medially; nostril surrounded by small scales. Auricular meatus one-half eye-slit.

Limbs long, toes slender, the dilatations well marked. The fore limb appressed reaches the groin; the hind limb extended attains the end of the muzzle. Fan little developed.

Above and below brilliant metallic green, with a few black dots along the vertebral line. Head and anterior part of sides, brown; a black V extending from the auricular openings, which are connected by a broad black band with the orbits. Another V extends towards the occiput from the limbs of the nuchal V, enclosing a narrow brown area with it. Top of muzzle and limbs blackish.

		M.
Total length .	.	0.108
Length to orbit	.	.005
" to ear .	.	.011
" to axilla .	.	.018
" to groin .		.0378
Width of head behind		.006
Length of hind foot .		.014

San José. Dr. Van Patten.

This small species is very abundant in Costa Rica, and is found also in Nicaragua.

53. ANOLIS PACHYPUS, Cope, sp. nov.

Tail slender, cylindric, with equal scales, swollen at the base. Scales of the abdomen smooth, those of the sides very small, on the back gradually enlarging to two or three largest and faintly keeled rows on the median line, which are much smaller than those of the belly. The head is rather short, its length equalling that of the tibia, and one-half greater than its width. Scales of top of head subequal in front, keeled; smaller and angular behind, covering a three-sided area behind the orbits, which is abruptly distinguished from the minute granules of the temples and nape. No facial rugæ distinct from canthus rostrales, but the frontal region concave from between the orbits to the middle of the muzzle. Superciliaries not larger than the scales of the five rows which separate them; frontal concavity with similar scales, and a little smaller than those of the three rows which separate them from the canthal row. Latter consisting of six scales, and continued on the edge of the eyebrow to near its middle in a manner unusual in the *Anolidæ*. Supraorbital region covered with projecting granules, except a single row of three or four small keeled supraoculars near the supraorbital border. Four rows between supraorbital series and occipital scale; eight loreal rows. Only one series of very small infralabials, the gulars running up to them in longitudinal lines. Meatus auditorius larger than occipital scale.

The feet are stout and clumsy; the wrist reaches the front of the orbit, and the end of the third toe of the hinder foot, the end of the muzzle. The digital dilatations are little or not more expanded distally than proximally, and the distal joints are covered with wide keeled scales above. Fan well developed.

	M.
Total length .	.135
Length to vent .	.047
" to axilla .	.020
" to tympanum .	.011
" of fore limb .	.022
" of fore foot .	.009
" of hind limb .	.043
" of hind foot .	.019
" of tibia · . .	.012

Color emerald-green, with a broad brown band from the orbit to the middle of the side, and a narrower one on each side of the sacrum. A green band from orbit to below tympanum, and a dark-brown band from orbit below the canthus rostralis. A dark-brown cross-band between the superciliary borders across the front. A deep brown spot behind the occiput, and a smaller one on the nape. Femur with a longitudinal black band behind, and an oblique one across the superior face. Tibia and forearm with a broad cross-band.

From the slope of the Pico Blanco; elevation not known.

A species markedly distinct in many respects, approaching the *A. scyphæus* in its few small supraocular scales.

54. ANOLIS OXYLOPHUS, Cope, spec. nov.

A species above medium size of the group with keeled ventral scales and without caudal crest or serra. The dorsal scales are distinctly larger than the lateral and about equal to the ventral. They are flat, subhexagonal, not imbricate, and have a median keel. There are at least twenty rows of equal size, those exterior to them graduating in size to the laterals. The scales of the upper surface of the head are very small, but flat, seven rows separating the rugal, and two the superciliary scuta. Small scales separate the rugal and canthal scuta. Occipital scute of moderate size, bounded laterally and in front by a number of scuta of the same size and form. Supraorbital disk composed of two rows of slightly keeled scuta with some small ones adjacent. Ten rows of loreals; 13–12 labials. Infralabials all very small and carinate. The canthus rostralis is distinct to near nostril. The facial ruga is remarkably prominent and acute, but not extending beyond the middle of the canthus. Auricular opening about one-fourth as long as the eye diameter. The form of the head is regular, and of good proportions; it is as long as the tibia. The middle of the third finger reaches the end of the nose, while the end of the longest toe reaches the middle of the orbit.

The color is a dark brown, the limbs and feet with pale cross-bands. A distinct whitish band extends from the scapular region to near the groin. Abdomen yellowish, with a broad brown border on each side. The fan is very large, but the color is altered by the alcohol.

		M.
Total length	.	.217
Length to vent	.	.076
" to groin	.	.071
" to axilla	. .	.035
" to ear	. . .	.019
" to orbit	. . .	.008
Width of head at angle of jaws	.	.011
Length of hind limb	. . . .	.060
" of hind foot	. . . .	.025

Both ♂ and ♀ specimens, the latter considerably smaller.

This species is allied to *A. pœcilopus*, Cope, and *A. concolor*, Cope (Proceed. Academy Phila., 1862, pp. 179–80). From the former it differs in the much more prominent frontal rugæ, the larger facial and especially posterior cephalic scales, and in the shorter hind legs. The latter differs in its obtuse ridges, larger facial and loreal scales, fewer labials, and other points.

55. ANOLIS INTERMEDIUS, Peters, Monatsber. K. Preuss. Acad. 1863, p. 143.
One specimen.

56. ANOLIS CAPITO, Peters, Monatsber. K. Preuss. Acad. Wiss. 1863, p. 142.
Five specimens from Old Harbor.

57. ANOLIS TESSELLATUS, O'Shaughnessy, Annals and Magaz. Nat. History, 1875, p. 279.
"Costa Rica."

58. POLYCHRUS MULTICARINATUS, Peters, Monatsberichte K. Preuss. Akad. 1869, p. 786. Bocourt, Miss. Sci. Mexique, Pl. XVII. fig. 8.
Unknown to me.

59. CORYTHOPHANES CRISTATUS, Merrem. Dum. Bibr. IV. p. 174.
Sipurio.

60. IGUANA RHINOLOPHA, Wiegmann, Herp. Mexicana, 44.
From the low country; Dr. Gabb.

61. CYCLURA ACANTHURA, Wiegmann, Herpetologia Mexicana, 42, t. 2.
San José; Dr. Van Patten.

62. BASILISCUS VITTATUS, Wiegm. Herpetologia Mexicana, p. 40, Pl. 15, 1834. *Corythæolus vittatus*, Kaup, Wiegmann. *Basiliscus*, Duméril. *Basiliscus nuchalis*, Cope, Proceed. Academy Philada., 1862, p. 181, (Southern form.)

Drs. Wiegmann, Wagler, Kaup, and Gray have described only the female of this species, and have established the genus *Corythophanes* on characters which belong to the female sex only. Prof. Duméril finds the male to possess the essential features of the genus *Basiliscus*, and I follow him in referring the species to that genus, as the specimens of the Smithsonian collection abundantly demonstrate the correctness of the view of the French herpetologist. The specimens from Nicaragua and Costa Rica differ from those of the north in their smaller size and larger dermal appendages. This variety I named *B. nuchalis*. The species ranges north to Vera Cruz.

Abundant. Numerous specimens from Sipurio. Mr. Gabb, like Dr. Sumichrast, states that this species runs over the surface of the water whose shores it frequents, like a spider.

The species of the genus *Basiliscus* known to me differ as follows:—

I. Dorsal and caudal rayed crests present.

Two dermal head-crests, the anterior narrow; both with large scales; four rows of interorbital scales; yellow spots; no longitudinal bands.   *B. plumifrons.*

One dermal head crest, with large scales; one row of interorbital scales; no longitudinal bands.   *B. mitratus.*

One expanded head crest with small scales; one row of interorbital scales; no longitudinal bands.   *B. guttulatus.*

One tassel-like head crest with small scales; more than one interorbital row; no longitudinal bands.   *B. goodridgii.*

II. A dorsal, no caudal rayed crest.

A single membranous head-crest covered with large scales; two or three interorbital rows; one or two longitudinal light bands on each side.   *B. vittatus.*

III. Neither dorsal nor caudal rayed crests.

A membranous head-crest of a horizontally elliptic form, covered with large scales; uniform green.   *B. seemannii.*

63. BASILISCUS PLUMIFRONS, sp. nov.

Represented in Mr. Gabb's collection by five male and one female specimens in fine preservation. It is more nearly allied to the *B. mitratus*, Daud., than to the *B. goodridgii* and *B. seemanii* of Gray, or the *B. vittatus*, Wiegmann. The abdominal scales are smooth, and both back and tail support elevated crests traversed by osseous rays. The head crest consists of a principal posterior portion

32

and an accessory anterior portion. The former commences above a point a little in front of the anterior margin of the meatus auditorius, and extends upwards and backwards to a subacute termination. The posterior border descends in an open sigmoid to the nape of the neck to a point a little behind the angle of the jaws. It is covered with large thin smooth scales, and its borders are acute. The anterior part of the helmet rises abruptly from a point in line with the posterior border of the orbit, its anterior border sloping backward to the obtuse extremity, which marks the basal third of the principal helmet. It is separated to the base from the latter by a fissure. The top of the head is covered with small scales, which are weakly or not at all keeled. The supraorbitals are smaller than the supraocular row, and weakly keeled; those covering the occipital protuberance are equal to them and nearly smooth. Three or four rows separate the superciliary series. Two distinct plates precede the nasal plate, the anterior in contact with the corresponding one of the opposite side. Labials, counting to the posterior border of the eye, seven above and seven below. The anterior three infralabials in contact with the inferior labials. Loreal rows four.

The dorsal scales are smaller than the ventral, but little larger than the lateral, and faintly keeled. Those of the upper surfaces of the limbs are as large as the abdominal and strongly keeled. The dorsal crest is highest behind the middle; its elevation exceeds that of the body by one-third; it is supported by fifteen rays. The scales covering it are smooth. The caudal crest is also elevated, and includes fifteen rays; it is covered by thin subequal scales, of which there are eight in a vertical row. Scales of the tail strongly keeled below, weakly keeled elsewhere. The fore foot is rather short; the ends of the metacarpals mark the muzzle when the limb is extended; the same point is reached by the ends of the basal phalanges of the extended hind limb.

Color everywhere green, becoming blue on the different crests. No longitudinal or transverse bands on the head, body, or throat. A row of distant round yellow spots from the axilla to the groin, and a similar row along the upper side of the back, which is wanting in some specimens. Various scales of the helmet and crests are paler than the others. Three vertical pale-bordered black spots on the dorsal crest, which may be obsolete in some individuals. Crested part of the tail green, the remainder yellowish, with brown rings to the end of the proximal two-thirds.

	M.
Total length (25.75 inches) .	. .655
Length to vent .	. .177
" to axilla	. .090

		M.
Length to ear	.	.045
" to orbit	.	.016
" of helmet	. .	.060
" of dorsal crest (vertical)	.	.045
Width between eyebrows	.	.021
Length of fore limb		.087
" of fore foot		.040
" of hind limb	.	.175
" of hind foot		.082
" of tibia	. . . . .	.057

Four of the specimens were taken at Sipurio.

Having had, through the attention of Professor A. Auguste Duméril, the opportunity of consulting the types preserved in the museum of the Jardin des Plantes, Paris, I can compare the present species with the original specimen of Seba, the type of the *B. mitratus* of Daudin. In that species, the anterior plume-shaped process of the front is wanting, and the helmet has a more posterior position. There is but one row of scales separating the superciliaries. There are five blackish transverse spots at the base of the dorsal crest, and two longitudinal pale stripes on the head and neck. These characters are borne out by two specimens procured by the expedition under Lieut. Michler from the Isthmus of Darien,[*] which offer other peculiarities also. Thus the caudal crest is chiefly covered by three longitudinal rows of large scales, there being but two or three of small ones below them. M. Bocourt (Miss. Sci. de Mexique, p. 127) states that the rays of the dorsal crest of the *B. mitratus* are 17–8, and of the caudal, 23; in the *B. plumifrons* they are constantly 15–15. The name of the species refers to the plume-shaped process in front of the helmet, which is constantly present. In the female the crests are wanting, and the helmet is very small, posterior, and without plume.

Mr. Gabb states that this species, like the other *Basilisci*, haunts the shores of rivers, where it lies on the bases of the leaves of the large canes which fringe the water. Its green color protects it from observation in this position, and it remains motionless when approached, so as to be readily caught by a noose of thread or hair.

64. SCELOPORUS MALACHITICUS, Cope, Proceed. Academy Philada., 1864, p. 178.

San Jose; Dr. Van Patten, C. N. Riotte.

* Vid. Proceed. Academy Philada., 1862, p. 356.

OPHIDIA.

SCOLECOPHIDIA.

65. HELMINTHOPHIS FRONTALIS, Peters, Monatsb. K. Preuss. Ak. 1861, p. 517.

Unknown to me.

Although no *Stenostomidæ* have yet been brought from Costa Rica, to my knowledge, yet they doubtless exist there, as the *Stenostoma albifrons* has been sent to the Smithsonian Institution from Panama by C. B. Adams, and a second species of the genus has been obtained in the western part of Tehuantepec by Dr. Francis Sumichrast. This appears to me to be new to science, and may be described as follows: I first compare it with those species of the genus which have but two labial plates, and no production nor angulation of the rostral plate, and in which the superciliaries are in contact with the first scale of the middle series, which is of the same form as those of the body. This species belongs also to those with large transverse temporal scales, and a narrow superciliary.

α. Superciliary in contact with first labial.
Last labial reaching one of the two temporals.   *S. albifrons.*
αα. Superciliary superior not reaching first labial.
   β. Last labial in contact with but one temporal.
      γ. Two temporals.
Rostral wide, nostril inferior; caudal scales 18; black.   *S. groutii.*
Rostral narrow; first labial not rising to eye; caudal scales 15; black lined.
                                                              *S. phenops.**
Rostral narrow; nostril terminal; first labial reaching eye; caudal scales 26;
   black lined.   *S. melanoterma.*
      γγ. One temporal.
Rostral narrow; first labial not rising to eye; caudal scales 15; black lined.
                                                              S. signatum.

---

* The STENOSTOMA PHENOPS from Tehuantepec is represented by numerous specimens, which are of small size and dark colors. Scales in 13 rows. The eye is distinct, and the nareal suture extends to the rostral plate. The lower surfaces are without marking, but the scales of the upper surface are black with pale borders. There are three white spots; one on the end of the rostral plate; one at the apex, and one on the under side of the tail. Total length, m. .156; tail, .009. The same species was obtained from near Coban, Guatemala, by Henry Hague.

The *Stenostoma melanoterma*, Cope, of the above table, was brought from Paraguay; see Proceed. Acad. Philada. 1862, p. 350. The *S. groutii*, Cope, is a new species, discovered by Dr. Alden S. Grout, near the Umvoti Mission, Zulu Country, South Africa. Scales in fourteen rows. The nasal plate is much narrowed at the labial border, and the first labial only rises as high as the nostril, which is half way from the edge of the lip to the orbit. Color uniform black, except a white spot at vent and one at apex of tail. Dedicated to Dr. Grout, who has sent numerous valuable specimens from the Zulu Country to Philadelphia.

β,β. Last labial united with two temporals.

First labial not reaching eye. *S. goudottii.*

ASINEA.

66. XIPHOSOMA ANNULATUM, sp. nov.*

Scales in fifty-four longitudinal rows on the body, and in forty-two at two inches behind the head. The top of the muzzle is covered with about fourteen small shields, of which two, a little larger than the rest, separate the nasals and bound the rostral. The latter plate is higher than wide, and has two long sutural borders on each side, and a short one on each side of the apex. Top of head covered with small smooth scales, of which twelve may be counted between the eyes, with superciliaries not distinguishable. The superior labial shields number fourteen, and are all pitted; only the posterior two-thirds of the inferior labials are pitted. Three loreal plates and one preocular; one series of scales separate the orbit from the labials, and bound the labial pits above. Gastrosteges 260; anal entire; urosteges 82.

Ash-colored, with darker ash-colored oval figures on each side. These are simply rings vertically placed, and they are occasionally connected on the median line above, where their color is more distinct. Head and lower surfaces uniform.

	M.
Total length	.755
Length of tail	.132
" to rictus of mouth	.079

This species exhibits the lip-pits and scutellation of the X. *caninum*, with the squamation and colors of the X. *hortulanum*.

---

* XIPHOSOMA RUSCHENBERGERII, sp. nov.

Scales in forty-seven rows on the body, and thirty-five rows two inches posterior to the head. Rostral plate higher than long. Superior labials all strongly pitted to the side of the rostral above, and on the posterior half below. The pits below the orbit are not separated from the latter by the projection of the row of scales above the labials, but these are enclosed in the pits which are thus continuous with the orbit. Top of the head covered with large scuta, the largest each subtriangular and separating the nasals. These are followed by a series of scuta above the canthus rostralis, which terminate in two or three large superciliary plates. The latter are separated by smaller scuta, the whole number between the orbits being in nine longitudinal rows. Only two loreals, and one preocular. Yellowish-brown, with occasional yellow scales above. Below bright yellow, on each side of the gastrosteges a series of brown spots. Tail black with yellow spots. Size of the X. *caninum*.

This species resembles the X. *hortulanum* more than the other species, but differs in the larger scales, large plates of the head, the pitted upper lips, and the coloration. There are fourteen rows of scales between the eyes in that species.

Obtained at Panama by Dr. W. S. W. Ruschenberger, President of the Academy, to whom the species is, with much pleasure, dedicated.

67. EPICRATES CENCHRIA, Linn., Dr. Van Patten.

68. BOA IMPERATOR, Daudin.

Not an uncommon species from the east coast to the foot of the mountains.

69. LEPTOGNATHUS ANNULATA, Günther, Annals and Magaz. Nat. Hist. 1872.

Not seen by me.

70. LEPTOGNATHUS ARGUS, Cope, sp. nov.

Body compressed; scales in fifteen rows, smooth, larger above than on the sides, the median row not abruptly larger than those adjoining it. Head wide, muzzle very short, orbit bounded in front by the loreal and prefontal scuta. Rostral plate triangular, as high as wide, very small; internasals small, prefontals large. Frontal and occipitals large, the former with parallel sides equal to the anterior border. Superior labials seven, orbit bounded by the fourth, fifth, and sixth. Inferior labials seven, the first, second, and third smaller than those that follow, the first pair not uniting behind the symphyseal. Gencial plates three pairs, the anterior two each longer than wide, the third quadrate, smaller. Postorbitals two, temporals 1–2. Gastrosteges 212; anal entire; urosteges 121.

				M.
Total length			. .	.345
Length of tail	.	.	. .	.104
" to rictus oris	.	.	. . . .	.007
Width of head behind	. .	. .	. . .	.007

Color above from the third row of scales greenish-ash, with two series of alternating light ocelli with black borders. Below, yellow to the third row of scales; the sides below that row with a series of black-edged ocelli like those of the back. Below, blackish speckled on the posterior half of the length. A large black-bordered ocellus on the nape. Head vermiculated with black; lips yellow, with black specks.

This species belongs to the same group of the genus as the L. anthracops, Cope. From Sipurio.

71. LEPTOGNATHUS PICTIVENTRIS, Cope, sp. nov.

Belonging to the same group of the genus as the L. argus, i. e. with the verte-bral series of scales not enlarged; scales smooth, and a pair of elongate colubriform gencial shields. It differs in the peculiarity that the front of the long gencials is in immediate contact with the wedge-shaped symphyseal. Scales in fifteen series, the lateral smaller. The muzzle is not so short as in the L. argus, but more as in L. nebulata. Internasals transverse triangles; frontal wide, occipitals long. Nasal undivided; orbit bounded by the prefontal above, the loreal medially and a pre-ocular below. Postoculars two, the inferior separating the seventh labials from the orbit. Superior labials eight, fifth and sixth bounding orbit, the sixth the longest, the seventh the widest plate, the four anterior higher than wide. Temporals 1–2. Inferior labials seven, four anterior smallest. Three pairs of gencials, two posterior pairs short, wide.

The colors of this species have been somewhat injured by spirits. The belly is yellow, with brown cross-bands on the anterior part of the body, the posterior part with large alternating brown spots. Back, at some points at least, crossed by continuations of the same. Throat and lips brown spotted. Urosteges 121.

This species differs from the last in the arrangement of the head plates both superior and inferior, as well as in the coloration.

72. LEPTOGNATHUS NEBULATA, Linn.
The dark colored variety.

73. DIPSAS GEMMISTRATUS, Cope, Proceed. Academy Philadelphia, 1861, p. 296; Van Patten.

74. DIPSAS OENCHOA, Linn.*

75. SIBON ANNULATUM, Linn.
With twenty-one rows of scales. From Old Harbor.

76. OXYRRHOPUS PLUMBEUS, Wied. *Brachyrhyton plumbeum*, Dum. Bibr.

I had occasion to observe on a former occasion that this species is a devourer of snakes, having received a specimen from Martinique which had swallowed the head and part of the body of a fer de lance (*Bothrops lanceolatus*). The present collection contains a specimen of m. 1.950 in length which had swallowed a *Her-*

---

* TRIMORPHODON COLLARIS, Cope, sp. nov.

Scales in twenty-three longitudinal rows; posterior gencials very short, separated by an intervening scale. Superior labials nine, fourth and fifth entering orbit. Loreals three; oculars 3–3; temporals 3–3–4–5. Head short and wide; internasal plates small; frontal in contact with superior preocular, and about as long as occipitals.

Body compressed, tail one-fifth the total. Ground color white (or ? yellow), crossed by sixteen black spots on the body in the type specimen (No. 148). The anterior three or four of these are longitudinally extended (the third, eleven scales long); the others are transverse diamond-shaped, the lateral apices extending well on the gastrosteges. Each is divided transversely by a narrow white line. Between each pair of spots is a small black spot on the border of the gastrosteges. Middle line of belly unspotted. Head black above, muzzle and lips yellow; a large projection of the yellow collar occupies a space on each side of the common parietal suture.

Orizaba, Vera Cruz; Dr. Sumichrast.

After examination of a large number of specimens of the genus *Trimorphodon*, Cope, I can recognize five species, viz.: *T. tau*, Cope; *T. upsilon*, Cope; *T. collaris*, Cope; *T. lyrophanes*, Cope, and *T. biscutatus*, Dum. Bibr. The last-named authors describe the *T. biscutatus* as having twenty-three series of scales, and I therefore on a previous occasion regarded it as unknown to me, and named the most common species of Central America and Mexico as *T. major*. I believe, however, that the latter is most probably the species of Duméril and Bibron, and that the number of scales given by those authors is not correct, as I find twenty-five and twenty-seven rows in the numerous specimens at my disposal.

petodryas carinatus of m. 1.970 in length, forty-two inches of the victim projecting from the mouth of its captor. As is necessarily the case, in both instances the captured snake had been seized by the muzzle, and so prevented from biting. Where venomous snakes are abundant the introduction of this harmless *Oxyrrhopus* would materially lessen their numbers. According to Mr. Gabb, it is a spirited and irascible species, making fight when attacked by man.

77. OXYRRHOPUS PETOLARIUS, Linn.

Red with subequidistant black half rings; muzzle black. Preocular not reaching frontal; two temporals in contact with postoculars. From Sipurio, the most northern locality for this snake.

78. DRYIOPHIS BREVIROSTRIS, Cope, Proceed. Academy Philadelphia, 1860, p. 555.

Similar to the type specimen, but with the scales nearly smooth. They are in fifteen series, the smaller lateral graduating into the larger dorsal. Muzzle rather short, nasal plate very narrow. Preocular reaching frontal. Labials six, eye resting on fourth, third entering the orbital ring. Postocular one, temporals 1–2. Seven inferior labials, first pair with long common suture, nearly equalling pregenials, which are longer than postgenials. Length m. .563; of tail .220. Color blue, paler below; lips yellowish. Body compressed, gastrosteges rounded.

From Gabb's collection. Typical examples from Dr. Van Patten.

79. DRYIOPHIS ACUMINATUS, Wied.

80. LEPTOPHIS ÆRUGINOSUS, Cope, sp. nov.

The genus *Leptophis* has been called *Ahaetulla* by Dr. Günther, and *Thrasops* by Dr. Hallowell. The former name was given by Dr. Gray in 1825 to the genus subsequently named *Dendrophis* by Boie, and, as I showed in 1860, must be retained for it. In Dr. Gray's list of species of *Ahaetulla*, not one is a member of the genus *Leptophis*. In the same year Bell gave the name *Leptophis* to a mixture of species of the two genera in question, commencing with an *Ahaetulla* (Gray). Having at one time adopted the rule of accepting the first species named by an author under a generic head as its type, I referred *Leptophis* to *Ahaetulla*, Gray, as a synonym, and employed *Thrasops*, Hallow., the name next in order of date. Having long since abandoned this position in favor of the more practicable one of regarding as the type of an author's genus the species remaining after the subtraction of all genera based on component species at prior or later dates, the name *Leptophis* remains for the species included by Bell, which are not *Ahaetullæ*. This course has been adopted by Duméril and Bibron.

Scales in fifteen series not keeled, but finely striate. Ventral scuta with very faint lateral angulations well separated from each other. Loreal present, subquadrate; preocular scarcely reaching frontal; postoculars two; temporals 1-2; nasal plate not elongate. Superior labials nine, fifth and sixth entering orbit. Inferior labials ten, six in contact with gencials, of which the posterior pair is the longer. Parietals bounded by small scales behind. Gastrosteges 146, anal divided; urosteges 142. Total length 405; of tail .155 m. Golden-brown above, or yellowish-green without the epidermis; vertebral line yellow on one row of scales for the anterior half of the body. Below blue, fading to yellowish on the gular region. A black band from eye along top of last superior labial.

From the low country.

81. LEPTOPHIS SATURATUS, Cope, sp. nov.

Scales in fifteen rows, one on each side of the median vertebral, weakly keeled; scales of the lateral rows wider than those of the median dorsal series. Gastrosteges not angulate. Head short and wide, eye large, its diameter equal to the length of the muzzle, or the width of the frontal with one superciliary plate. Internasals and prefontals wider than long, the frontal, superciliaries, and parietals wide for the genus, the last openly emarginate behind. Nasals not elongate, the anterior the higher; loreal present, nearly twice as long as high; orbitals 1-2, preorbital nearly reaching frontal. Temporals 1-2, the anterior large. Labials nine above, the fifth and sixth bounding the orbit; ten inferior labials, six in contact with the gencials. Gastrosteges 160; anal divided; urosteges 133.

		M.
Total length		.880
Length of tail		.340
" to rictus oris		.022
" to orbit		.007

Color in spirits, indigo blue, very dark on head and vertebral rows of scales. Lips dark green, a blackish shade above the labial plates from the orbits posteriorly.

The last maxillary tooth of this species is much longer than those that precede it without interval.

The wide and depressed head as well as the smooth scales and color, distinguish this species from the L. mexicanus, D. B. The muzzle, and hence the scuta, are less elongate than in the L. depressirostris, Cope.

One specimen from Sipurio.

82. LEPTOPHIS MEXICANUS, Dum. Bibr.

Valley of Costa Rica; Dr. Van Patten.

83. LEPTOPHIS PRÆSTANS, Cope, Proceed. Academy Philada. 1868, p 309.

Sipurio.

34

84. DENDROPHIDIUM MELANOTROPIS, Cope, sp. nov.

The genus *Dendrophidium* was first defined by the writer in the Proceedings Philada. Academy, 1860, p. 561. Its dentition is isodont and coryphodont, in which, with its two preoculars, it resembles *Bascanium* (*Masticophis*). From this genus its strongly keeled scales separate it. Its type is *Herpetodryas dendrophis* of Schlegel: a second species is *H. brunneus*, Gthr., from Equador.

Posterior maxillary tooth a little longer and much stouter than the anterior teeth, the three or four preceding teeth forming a graded series of intermediate size. Scales in seventeen series, all keeled excepting the inferior two on each side; the lateral scales wider than the median; the keels of the row on each side of the vertebral stronger than those of the others. Gastrosteges not angulate. Head elevated, eye large, its diameter one and a half times in the length of the muzzle, and equal to the width of the frontal and one superciliary shield. Superior labials nine, the fourth, fifth, and sixth entering the orbit. These plates are rather small to the eighth, which is much longer than high, and the ninth, which is higher than long. Rostral plate not protuberant, wider than high; postnasal higher than prenasal. Loreal much longer than high, angulate above owing to the oblique suture with the superior preocular. Preoculars two, the superior wide, not reaching the frontal; the inferior much smaller, resting on the middle of the fourth superior labial; on one side united with the superior preocular. Postoculars two, equal, narrow and elevated. Temporals 2–2, short and deep. Internasals longer than wide; prefontals longer than wide; frontal bell-shaped, wide in front, contracted behind; superciliaries rather narrow. Parietals wide, remarkably short, their greatest length equal to that of the frontal, less than that of the superciliary; their posterior borders convex, including a notch. Scales behind them smooth. The scales of the body are biporous, the pores situated at a distance in front of the apex of the scale, and dark pigmented. Gastrosteges 152; anal divided; urosteges 94.

Color above and including the external fourth of the gastrosteges green; the skin between the scales and the keels of the median three dorsal rows, black; lower surfaces light yellow.

		M.
Total length . .		. 1.240
Length of tail . .		. .365
" to rictus oris .		. .035
Width between supercilia		.072
Diameter of eye		.008

This fine species is of aberrant character; it resembles in size and coloration the *Thrasops præstans*, Cope, of the same region.

85. DRYMOBIUS MARGARITIFERUS, Schlegel.
    San José.

86. DRYMOBIUS BODDAERTII, Seetz.
    Talamanca and San José.

87. HERPETODRYAS CARINATUS, L.

Scales in ten longitudinal rows on the front, and eight on the posterior part of the body, keeled and about as large as the parietal scuta excepting the first row on each side, which is smaller and smooth. The keels of the two median rows are stronger, and become very prominent on the posterior part of the body, forming together an elevated flat-topped ridge, which gradually disappears on the tail, so that the scales of its distal half are smooth. The third row of scales is smooth on the posterior part of the body. There is usually a single pore at the end of the scale, but sometimes it is wanting. Nine upper labial scuta, the fourth, fifth, and sixth bounding the orbit. Loreal nearly as high as long; oculars 1–2, the posteriors equal, the anterior not reaching the frontal. Last upper labials not elevated; temporals 2–2. Parietals wide, short, as long as superciliaries, bounding a deep notch behind. Gastrosteges 162; anal divided; urosteges 135.

Color black above, below yellow, the former encroaching on the latter and obliterating it on the posterior part of the belly, and on the tail.

	M.
Total length	1.970
Length of tail	.780
" of head to rictus oris	.042

The only specimen of this snake was taken from the stomach of an *Oxyrrhopus plumbeus* of one foot less length. The tail and a portion of the body projected from the mouth of its captor. From the low country.

88. HERPETODRYAS GRANDISQUAMIS, Peters; *Spilotes grandisquamis*, Peters, Monatsberichte K. Akad. Berlin, 1868, p. 451.

89. SPILOTES PULLATUS, Linn.; *Coluber variabilis*, Wied.; *Spilotes variabilis*, Dum. Bibr.

90. SPILOTES CORAIS, Cuv., Günther, Catal. Colub. Snakes Brit. Mus. 1858, p. 98; subspecies MELANURUS, Dum. Bibr.

This form ranges from Panama to northern Mexico, preserving the oblique black mark on the neck and the black tail. When the black involves the entire body and head, it becomes the subspecies *S. c. erebennus* (*Spilotes erebennus*, Cope;

Coluber obsoletus, Holbr., not Say).   This subspecies extends from the Rio Grande to Alabama.

San José and Talamanca.

91. SPILOTES CHRYSOBRONCHUS, sp. nov.

Scales in twenty-five series, all smooth excepting the row next the vertebral, which is weakly keeled.   Head flat; orbit large, contained 1.66 times in side of muzzle, and 2.25 times in space between their superior borders.   Rostral plate broad as high, not protuberant; nasals large, subequal.   Loreal small, longer than high; preocular 1–2, the anterior wide, not reaching the frontal.   Postoculars subequal, bounded by two temporals.   Internasals wider than long, frontal longer than wide in front, little shorter than parietals; latter rounded behind.   Temporals 2–2–2, one long, one bounding two upper temporals below.   Superior labials seven (a partial division into eight on one side of one specimen); third, fourth, and fifth bounding the orbit.   All of them low, the sixth not triangular, the seventh on both sides of two specimens, more than twice as long as any of the others.   Twelve inferior labials, eight in contact with the genials; first pair large, second to sixth narrow and deep; eleventh narrow and longitudinal.   Genials elongate subequal.   Gastrosteges 220; anal entire; urosteges 117.   Scale-pores in pairs.

Color brown, the scales dotted with lighter, head darker; one or more borders of the scales black.   Upper lip, throat, and anterior part of the belly, yellow remainder of lower surfaces passing from brown to black below the tail.   The only markings are small black dots on the two lower rows of scales, commencing at the neck and extending to the end of the anterior fourth of the length.

		M.
Total length . .	.	. 1.670
Length of tail . . .	.	. .422
" to canthus of mouth	.	. .040

From the coast region.

This species is evidently near to the *S. fasciatus*, Peters.   There are many trivial differences to be found in the description of the latter, and a few of importance.   The frontal of *S. chrysobronchus* cannot be said to be "very wide," and it is not in contact with the preorbitals, as in *S. fasciatus*.   The parietals are not truncate, and the dorsal scales are not so much keeled as in the latter.   In *S. chrysobronchus* the number of gastrosteges exceeds that of the urosteges by 103; in *S. fasciatus* by only 59.   The coloration is materially different, the latter having black cross-bands, spots, etc.

92. LIOPHIS EPINEPHELUS, Cope, Proceed. Academy, Philada., 1862, Feb.

San José; Dr. Van Patten.

93. CONOPHIS LINEATUS, Dum. Bibr.; *Tomodon lineatus*, Dum. Bibr.; *Conophis lineatus*, Cope, Proc. Acad. Philada. 1871, p. 204.

San José; Dr. Van Patten.

There are five species of this genus, distributed from Costa Rica to Yucatan, which differ as follows:—

I. Seven upper labials;

a. Temporals in two rows; loreal higher than long.

Body without bands, but faint traces of them on first, third, and seventh rows of scales.   *C. vittatus*, Peters.

Body banded on third and eighth rows.   *C. sumichrastii*, Cope.

Var: second row not covered by lateral band; dorsal bands distinct.

Subspecies *sumichrastii*.

Var: second to fifth and eighth to eighth covered by lateral and median band.

Subspecies *viduus*.

II. Eight upper labials.

a. Two rows of temporals.

Loreal higher than long. Six longitudinal bands, the lower on the first row of scales, two dorsal, none on the belly; head brown yellow banded.

C. pulcher, Cope.

Loreal long, or longer than high; no bands except a short one from muzzle through eye.   *C. concolor*, Cope.

a. One row of temporals in front; large ones behind.

Loreal longer than high; bands on all the scales except those of the fifth row on each side.   *C. lineatus*, D. & B.

The *Conophis sumichrastii*, Cope, has been found by M. Sumichrast in the western part of Tehuantepec, and near Guadalaxara by I. I. Major. The subspecies *C. s. viduus* is also from Tehuantepec, from M. Sumichrast. It is a mimetic analogue of *Coniophanes piceivittis*, Cope, from the same place.

94. CONIOPHANES FISSIDENS, Günther, Catal. Col. Snakes B. M., 36 (*Coronella*).

Sipurio and·Old Harbor, abundant.

I am acquainted with seven species of this genus from the region north of Panama and south of Coahuila. They may be readily distinguished as follows:—

I. Scales in twenty-five longitudinal rows.

Superior labials eight; three broad longitudinal black bands. *C. piceivittis*, Cope.

II. Scales in twenty-one rows (labials 8).

Sides dark above; a broad dorsal band; light lines on the sides of the nape; belly unspotted.   *C. punctigularis*, Cope.

35

Sides shaded above; no dorsal bands nor abdominal spots; light lines on sides of
nape.   *C. fissidens*, Gthr.

Lines very indistinct, none on nape; two rows of brown spots on belly.
                                                              C. bipunctatus, Gthr.

III. Scales in nineteen rows.

Labials seven or eight; sides dark, a narrow vertebral line; a light band behind
each orbit.   *C. proterops*, Cope.

Labials eight; sides dark, a broad dorsal band from head; a light band from end
of muzzle above eye.   *C. imperialis*, B. & G.

Labials seven; frontal plate wide; head black, body red.   *C. lateritius*, Cope.

95. PLIOCERCUS DIMIDIATUS, Cope, Proceed. Academy Philada. 1865, p. 190.

Tail two-fifths the total length; urosteges 120, nearly equal in number to the
gastrosteges—127. Scales in seventeen rows, the median scarcely narrowed. Head
very distinct, flat, muzzle truncate. Top of rostral shield round, curved back on
the upper plane. Internasals very small; lateral borders of frontal (vertical) nearly
parallel, a little shorter than anterior. Occipitals large. Temporals, 1 very narrow,
1 pentagonal, 2. Loreal nearly a rhomb, lower than postnasal; preoculars three,
upper not reaching frontal, lower cut from labial. Superior labials nine, fifth and
sixth entering orbit; postoculars two, superior in contact with occipital only.
Nine inferior labials, sixth largest; gencials equal. Teeth equal.

Red, crossed by fourteen black rings on the body, and eight and a part on the
tail. These are separated by nearly equal spaces below, and rather narrower (3½
scales) above. A black space involves the nape to the tips of the occipital and
last upper labial plates and all the last lower, and does not meet on the jugulum.
The remainder of the head above black except the anterior part of the frontal
and the first, second, and third superior labial shields. Lower labials bordering
anterior gencials, with symphyseal, black.

Costa Rica; sent by Charles N. Riotte, correspondent of the Smithsonian
Institution: Mus. No. 6363.

96. RHADINÆA DECORATA, Gth. l. c. 35 (*Coronella*).

Sipurio; abundant.

The genus *Rhadinæa* is nearly coextensive with *Enicognathus*, Jan, and *Ablabes*,
Günther. *Ablabes* of Dum. Bibr. was, however, established on the *Coronella rufula*
of Schlegel, which has the prolonged series of gastric hypapophyses, and is therefore quite different, while *Henicognathus* is characterized by a peculiar structure of
the mandible, which, so far as I am aware, occurs in only one American species,
the *H. annulatus*, D. B. Consequently the majority of species attached to this

genus belong to *Rhadinæa*, as the *E. melanocephala*, D. B., etc. In the description of this last species three are mingled, as I have ascertained both from a reading of the same and from an examination of the originals in Mus. Paris. One of these is our *R. obtusa*, the other is the true *R. melanocephala*, and the third is a species which I described under the name of *Lygophis nicagus*, Cope. Duméril and Bibron give both the Island of Guadaloupe and Brazil as habitats of their species. I suspect, however, that the specimen of *R. obtusa* was accidentally introduced into the jar containing the other two, and that it is confined to South America, where it is not uncommon. It is figured by Jan in his "Iconographie" as the second specimen of *R. melanocephala*. His first specimen of the same as figured is our *Lygophis nicagus*, a serpent with a diacranterian dentition. The true *R. melanocephala* is probably confined to Guadaloupe and the neighboring islands.

It is probable that the *Dromicus tæniatus*, Ptr., *D. godmanii*, and *D loreatus* of Günther, belong to this genus, as does the *D. ignitus*, Cope. The posterior tooth is a little longer than the anterior in most of the species, and when one or two teeth in advance of it are broken off or shed, the result may resemble the diacranterian type of dentition characteristic of *Dromicus*. Dr. Günther expressly states that the dentition of his *D. loreatus* is not of that type. The species of *Rhadinæa* may then be distinguished as follows, with the premise that the characters of those above named are only known to me from the descriptions of the authors who made them known:—

I. Scales in twenty-one rows.
Loreal longer than high; three principal bands, with other less prominent ones
  between them.   *R. godmanii.**

II. Scales in nineteen rows.
Loreal longer than high; nine longitudinal bands.   *R. serperastra*, Cope.

III. Scales in seventeen rows.
  a. One preocular.
Loreal higher than long; sides with dark line above; a black-edged pale band
  from eye to side; head pale, lips spotted.   *R. vermiculaticeps.†*
Loreal high as long; three broad brown bands; the light ground color extending
  to the eye; lips unspotted.   *R. fulcivittis.‡*

* *Dromicus godmannii*, Günther.
† *Tæniophis vermiculaticeps*, Cope.
‡ RHADINÆA FULVIVITTIS, Cope, sp. nov.
  Head small, not very distinct from body. Frontal a little longer than the suture from it to the nasal, and a little shorter than common suture of occipitals, two-thirds as wide as long.

Loreal longer than high; a narrow lateral and broad (sometimes divided) dorsal band; the included band reaching side of muzzle; urosteges 90–108.

*R. tœniata.**

Sides with dark border above; an oblique yellow band from eye crossing the last labial; urosteges 60.   *R. lachrymans.†*

A dorsal band; a yellow band encircling head on labials and nape; a yellow band through orbit to nape.   *R. loreata.‡*

    aa. Two preoculars.

Sides dark above, with a superior pale border, which becomes a yellow band on each side of head to orbit; no dorsal band; lips unspotted.   *R. ignita.§*

Sides dark above, with superior pale border; two yellow spots on each side of occiput and nape; urosteges 90.   *R. decorata.‖*

97. RHADINÆA SERPERASTRA, Cope, Proceed. Acad. Philada. 1871, p. 212.

This species agrees with those regarded as typical, when the genus was first defined (see Proc. Academy N. Sci. 1868, p. 132). That is, the teeth are equal, the scales smooth and poreless, the anal plate divided, the nasals two, loreal one, and oculars 1–2.

In this serpent the scales are in nineteen series. Superior labials eight, not elevated, fourth and fifth bounding eye. Temporals 1–2–3. Internasals transverse, narrow; postnasal larger than prenasal. Frontal wide, superciliary suture shorter than anterior, total length exceeding that of common parietal suture. Loreal square; geneials subequal. Gastrosteges 164; anal 2, urosteges 78.

Dark brown with six longitudinal yellow or white lines, of which the first and second are brightest. The second dark band is wider than the first and vertebral; and like the third is partly divided by a faint white line. Another white line on each side is produced by a series of dark spots on the ends of the gastrosteges. Labial plates black, yellow spotted. Head dark brown above with a pale shade across frontal and two just behind parietals. Chin and belly yellowish.

Rostral small, low; postnasal higher than long; loreal as high as long. Superior labials eight, seventh highest; temporals 1–1. Inferior labials ten, sixth largest, in contact with middle of postgeneials. Scales poreless. Gastrosteges 177; anal divided; urosteges 91.

Color above fulvous, below fulvous-yellow. The three brown bands extend from the end of the nose to near the end of the tail; the lateral involves the fourth and the half of each adjacent row of scales, and is black edged; the dorsal is three and two half scales wide, and is also black edged. The brown is paler on top of the head, and the ground color is a narrow yellow band to the eye. Lips yellow, like the lower surfaces unspotted.

From Orizaba, Vera Cruz; obtained by Dr. Sumichrast; No. 7075 Mus. Smithsonian.

   * *Dromicus*, Peters.   † *Lygophis*, Cope.

   ‡ *Dromicus*, Günther.   § *Dromicus*, Cope.

   ‖ *Coronella*, Günther.

98. ERYTHROLAMPRUS VENUSTISSIMUS, Wied.

Sipurio.

99. XENODON ANGUSTIROSTRIS, Peters, Monatsber. K. Preuss. Akad., Berlin.

Sipurio.

100. STENORHINA VENTRALIS, Dum. Bibr., Erp. Gen. vii. 867.

Several specimens from Old Harbor.

The genera related to *Stenorhina* are numerous, and their characters may be tabulated as follows:—

I. Internasal plates wanting.

　　a. Rostral produced backwards to the frontal.

Nasals and first labial confluent.　　　　　　　　　　　　*Ficimia*, Gray.

　　aa. Rostral not separating prefontals.

Nasals confluent with first labial; anal entire; prefontals in contact medially.

　　　　　　　　　　　　　　　　　　　　　　　　　　　Sympholis, Cope.

Nasals and first labial distinct; anal divided.　　　　　*Conopsis*, Günth.

II. Internasals confluent with nasal plates.

Dentition glyphodont.　　　　　　　　　　　　　　　*Stenorhina*, D. B.

Dentition isodont; rostral shovel-like.　　　　　　　*Chilomeniscus*, Cope.

III. Internasals and prefontals distinct.

　　a. Internasals separated by backward production of the rostral.

Nasals confluent with first labial.　　　　　　　　　　　*Gyalopium*, Cope.

　　aa. Prefontals separated by forward production of the frontal.

Nasals one, distinct from labial.　　　　　　　　　　　　*Toluca*, Kenn.

　　aaa. Prefontals in contact medially.

　　　　β. Dentition isodont.

　　　　　　γ. Subcaudal scutella divided.

No loreal; anal divided; two nasals; rostral produced.　　*Geagras*, Cope.*

---

* GEAGRAS REDIMITUS, Cope, sp. nov.

Head not distinct; muzzle depressed, projecting much beyond the mouth, so that the first superior labial is mostly inferior. Superior face of rostral as wide as length of prefontals; that of internasals narrower, both pairs much wider than long. Frontal large, wide, and produced behind; parietals as long as frontal, narrowed, bifurcate behind, the notch occupied by a large scale. Superciliary plate small. Nasals elongate, very distinct, the posterior angle produced to the preocular, on one side cut off, forming a loreal. Oculars 1–1, the posterior barely touching by its posterior angle the anterior angle of the single temporal. Labials five above, the eye resting on the middle of the third, which with the fifth is the longest. Inferior labials six, of which three are in contact with the pregencials, and the fourth and largest with the short post-gencials. The symphyseal is wide, and in full contact with the pregencials; postgencials not

A loreal; anal entire; two nasals; rostral produced.   *Cemophora*, Cope.

A loreal; anal divided; one nasal; rostral much produced.   *Chionactis*, Cope.

A loreal; anal divided; two nasals, rostral obtuse, not produced.   *Sonora*, B. & G.

ω. Subcaudal scutella entire.

Rostral produced; scuta normal.   *Rhinochilus*, B. & G.

β,*β*. Dentition glyphodont.

Rostral little produced; nasal distinct, undivided.   *Ogmius*, Cope.

IV. Prefontals continuous on the middle line.

Internasals distinct; rostral produced.   *Ligonirostra*, Cope.

Internasals medially united.   *Prosymna*, Gray.

The preceding genera are all Mexican, Sonoran, or from adjoining regions, excepting *Ligonirostra* and *Prosymna* (African). *Ligonirostra*, Cope (Amer. Journ. Sci. Arts, 1863) was formerly called *Temnorhynchus* by Smith, but that name was preoccupied.

There are only two species of *Stenorhina*, but several subspecies, which differ as follows:—

Eight inferior labials, fifth largest. No loreal; narrow cross-bands.

                                     S. kennicottiana, Cope.

Seven inferior labials, fourth largest. Seventeen rows scales; temporals 1–2.

                                     S. deyenhardtii, Berth.

Subspecies I. Adults plumbeous-brown; no loreal; young with broad cross-bands.   *S. d. ventralis*, D. B.

Subsp. II. A loreal; scales above the third row with a black tip; ground color pale brown.   *S. d. apiata*, Cope.

Subsp. III. Loreal present or absent; five black longitudinal bands on a light brownish ground.   *S. d. freminvillei*, D. & B.

The *S. d. apiata* is from Tehuantepec, from Sumichrast.

101. TANTILLA MELANOCEPHALA, Linn., Dum. Bibron, vii. p. 859.

From Van Patten's collection.

separated from each other by scales. Scales of the body smooth, poreless, and in fifteen longitudinal rows. Gastrosteges 118; anal double; urosteges 25.

Color very pale yellow, each scale, excepting those of the first row, with a brown apical spot, which is in all except the two outer of these, continued to the base of the scale as a brown line. Head above dark brown, with an oval yellowish ellipse surrounding the middle portions, passing round the muzzle and superciliary, and through the length of the parietal plates as a wide band. Below unspotted. Total length m. 166; length to rictus oris, .005; of tail, .020.

Found by Dr. Francis Sumichrast on the west side of the State of Tehuantepec, Mexico, and sent by him to the Smithsonian Institution (No. 8).

To the above description I add that the *Toluca frontalis*, Cope, from Colima, is congeneric with this species in all technical characters.

102. TANTILLA ARMILLATA, Cope, sp. nov.; *Tantilla melanocephala*, var. Cope, Proceed. Acad.
Philada. 1871, p. 205.

Form slender; scales in fifteen longitudinal rows. Rostral plate not protuberant; prefontals three times as long as internasals, equalling the parietal suture of the frontal. Frontal wide, considerably shorter than parietals. Nasals little notched below, the posterior reaching the preocular. Seventh superior labial much the largest; temporals 1–1, the anterior bordering the postoculars. Inferior labials six, first pair slightly united, four in contact with geneials, fourth largest, elongate, touching both geneials. Gastrosteges 166; anal divided; urosteges 50.

Above chocolate-brown; head and nape for five scales, black, with a yellow spot in the individual described, on the end of the muzzle, on the posterior part of each parietal plate; and two on the lip behind the eye, and one below the nostril. The black is bordered behind by a yellow collar of two scales width, which is also bordered by black behind except where it sends off on the third and fourth rows of scales on each side a narrow light band which extends to the tail. Below this, and on the median row of scales, is a narrow brown line. Below immaculate.

Middle Costa Rica; Dr. Van Patten.

The species of *Tantilla* may be distinguished as follows:—

I. Superior labials six; orbitals 1–1.

Muzzle produced; preorbital not in contact with superciliary nor nasal; three
longitudinal bands.   *T. calamarina*, Cope.

Muzzle less produced; preorbital in contact with superciliary and nasal; temporal
one; three bands.   *T. bimaculata*, Cope.[*]

Temporals two; no bands.   *T. gracilis*, B. & G.

II. Superior labials seven; orbitals 1–1.

Coloration uniform.   *T. planiceps*, Blainv.

III. Superior labials seven; two postoculars.

α. Postnasals in contact with preocular, or nearly so.

---

[*] TANTILLA BIMACULATA, Cope, sp. nov.

Scales in fifteen rows. Rostral strongly protuberant beyond mouth. Nasals little notched below by first labial; postnasal barely or quite reaching preocular. Frontal large, longer than suture to rostral, not presenting an angle forwards; superciliaries not reduced; parietals about as long as the frontal. One temporal barely touching postocular; fifth upper labial highest. Five inferior labials, first pair widely separated, only three in contact with geneials, third largest in contact with both geneials. Gastrosteges 130; anal double; urosteges 34.

Color light brown with three darker narrow longitudinal bands. Top of head dark colored in continuation of the middle band; on each side of the occipital plate behind a large yellow spot. Below immaculate.

This well-marked species was found near Mazatlan by Mr. Bischoff, and is No. 6834 of the Smithsonian Catalogue.

β. Posterior labials elevated, separated from parietals by one temporal.

Form slender; a yellow, black-bordered collar near parietal plates.   *T. miniata*, Cope.

ββ. Posterior labials elevated, bounded above by two temporals.

Labials higher; first inferior labials separate; black with wide yellow collar.

T. moesta, Gthr.

Frontal narrower; posterior labials higher; body banded.   *T. melanocephala*, Linn.

Frontal wider; posterior labials lower; body uniform red.   *T. rubra*,* Cope.

βββ. Posterior labials low, bounded above by two temporals.

γ. Inferior labials of first pair in contact on the middle line.

Postnasal very small; collar far behind head; body banded; urosteges 51.

T. armillata, Cope.

Postnasal large; collar crossing parietal scuta; body unicolor.   *T. coronata*, B & G.

γγ. Inferior labials separated by symphyseal.

Urosteges 67; postnasal large, bounded below by first labial; a yellow collar.

T. reticulata, Cope.

Urosteges 57; postnasal chiefly bounded by second labial; head black, no collar.

T. nigriceps, Kenn.

Urosteges 39; first labial rising to nostril; head and body uniform.

T. canula,† Cope.

---

* TANTILLA RUBRA, Cope, sp. nov.

Scales poreless, in fifteen rows. Rostral plate little prominent; frontal wide, its anterior borders longer than its superciliary, and forming together an anterior angle. Superciliaries well developed; parietals much longer than frontal, notched behind. Nasals strongly notched below for the first labial; the postnasal barely touching the large preocular by its angle. Last three labials elevated, the seventh most so; temporals 1–1, the anterior in contact with postoculars. Only six inferior labials, first pair in contact, the fourth largest, elongate, and in contact with gencials of both pairs. Gastrosteges 149; anal divided; tail injured. Length of head and body m. .310. Color red; top of head black, followed by a yellow collar which involves the extremities of the parietal plates, and is followed by a black collar three scales wide. A pale spot below nostril and one on lip behind orbit. From Dr. Sumichrast, from Japana, Tehuantepec.

† TANTILLA CANULA, Cope, sp. nov.; *Tantilla vermiformis*, "Hallow.;" Cope, Proceed. Academy Philada. 1866, p. 126.

This small species is represented by two specimens (Nos. 413 and 737) taken by Arthur Schott in Yucatan, while attached to the Comision Scientifica under the direction of Governor Illaregui. Comparison with four of the *T. vermiformis* of Hallowell establishes the specific difference of the two in a satisfactory manner.

Scales in fifteen rows without apical pores; muzzle rather wide, but projecting beyond the mouth. Internasals and prefontals narrow, transverse, frontal rather small, longer than suture to rostral, to which it presents an angle. Superciliaries rather large; parietals longer than frontal, notched behind. Temporals 1–1; eye over suture between third and fourth labials; seventh labial the largest. Postgencials short, in contact with each other. Fourth labial below, the largest, in contact with pre- and postgencials. Color leaden, darker above. Head shields with paler borders and centres. Gastrosteges 110; anal divided; urosteges 37. Total length m. .172; of tail .037.

Urosteges 25; nasals not interrupted by first upper labial; head dark with a pale occipital spot. *T. vermiformis*, Hallow.

    aa. Postnasals separated from preocular by a wide space.

No loreal; last upper labial larger than sixth; body above with black and white half-rings. *T. semicincta*, D. & B.

A loreal; last upper labial smaller than sixth; body with complete black and white rings. *T. atrocincta*, D. & B.

103. MICRODROMUS VIRGATUS, Günther, Ann. Magaz. Nat. Hist. 1872, Pl. IV.

    Unknown to me.

104. NINIA ATRATA, Hallow.; *Streptophorus drozii*, Dum. Bibr.

    San José; Dr. Van Patten.

105. NINIA SEBÆ, D. & B.; subspecies MACULATA, Peters, Monatsber. K. Preuss. Akad. 1861, p. 924. Subspecies TESSELLATUS, Cope.

This distinct color variety resembles the typical in squamation, as in the nineteen rows of scales all keeled, seven superior labials with the third and fourth entering the orbit, and in the four lower labials in contact with the gensials. The color above is a rosy brown, marked with numerous transverse bands of black with zigzag borders, as the color covers entire scales. Neck of the same ground color; head above brown. Lower surfaces black, with square ? red spots on the gastrosteges. This portion of the coloration is quite distinct from that of the *N. s. maculata*, or other varieties.

106. CONTIA PACHYURA, sp. nov.

Scales smooth, in seventeen longitudinal rows, generally poreless, sometimes with one pore. Head rather elongate, rostral plate not prominent; interuasals wider than long; prefontals long as wide. Frontal rather elongate, but shorter than the parietals. Nasals oblique; loreal large, higher than long, encroaching on the single preocular, which does not reach the frontal. Postoculars two, smooth, subequal; temporals 1-1. Superior labials eight, the fourth and fifth entering orbit, the posterior rather low. Genials equal, rather elongate. The tail is long, entering the total length three and three-fifth times, and is thickened to near the end. Gastrosteges 133; urosteges 50. Total length m. .335.

The color is black, the lower lateral rows of scales with a rufous shade. Scales of the first row with gray tips. Head blackish-brown, a black line from eye above labials; latter yellowish, unspotted. Belly yellowish, each scutum with a black extremity.

    From Sipurio.

37

This species is allied to the *C. calligaster*, differing in its physiognomy and coloration as well as in some technical characters. Thus the loreal plate is larger and differently formed, and the tail is longer and stouter. It is less than one-fifth the length in the *C. calligaster*.

107. CONTIA CALLIGASTER, Cope, sp. nov.

Form stout, head little distinct. Teeth gradually increasing in length to the posterior, which is smooth. Scales smooth, poreless; one nasal plate, a subquadrate loreal, one pre- and two postoculars. Muzzle narrowed; side of frontal plate longer than the front, not reaching the preocular. Superior labials seven, third and fourth bounding orbit; temporals 1-1-2. Inferior labials eight, fourth and fifth largest, first barely in contact behind symphyseal. Scales acuminate, in seventeen rows. Gastrosteges 152, anal double; the urosteges 46. Pre- and postgenials equal.

Color above dark brown, with a narrow vertebral black band. Two lateral paler bands, on the first and second and fourth and fifth rows of scales, the space between black. A black band along the ends of the gastrosteges; belly yellow, except a series of black crescents on the median front of each suture. Labials broadly black bordered. Middle line of tail below black. In a second specimen there is an additional superior labial in front of the orbit, and the temporals are 1-2-2. The lateral light lines are wide and indistinct, and the entire base of each gastrostege is black.

From the Pico Blanco.

108. CATOSTOMA PSEPHOTUM, Cope, sp. nov.

Scales in seventeen longitudinal rows, keeled except the inferior. Form rather slender, the head moderately distinct. Maxillary teeth extending as far as the posterior border of the first upper labial. Front somewhat convex, internasals four-sided. Frontal with convex anterior suture, and lateral and two posterior sutures subequal. Orbit bounded by the prefrontal and large loreal; nasal undivided. Postorbitals two, temporals 1-2-2. Superior labials six, fourth immediately under orbit, but the third touching it; sixth longest. Inferior labials six, first pair joined behind symphyseal; all these, with the pregenials, tuberculate (in one specimen). A pair of short postgenials. Median keels stronger than the others; tail with triangular section. Gastrosteges 162; anal entire; urosteges 73. Color above uniform black; below black with the half or less of an occasional scutum red, forming a tesselated pattern; but few spots on the urosteges.

	M.
Total length	. .480
Length of tail . .	. .128
" to rictus oris .	. .010
Width of head behind	. .008

109. CATOSTOMA DOLICHOCEPHALUM, Cope; *Colobognathus dolichocephala*, Cope, Proceed. Acad. Philada. 1871, p. 211.

Scales in thirteen longitudinal series, carinate to the urosteges on the tail, to the first row of scales on the posterior, and to the second row on the anterior part of the body. Head elongate conic, scarcely distinct from the neck. Internasals very small, prefrontals very long. Frontal wide, openly angulate in front, with superciliary margins distinct from the parietal; latter plates well developed. Superior labials six, second bounding nasal and loreal; third a little, fourth largely in the eye, fifth longer than high, in contact with parietal. One temporal above sixth labial, which is higher than long. Inferior labials six, second and third minute, fourth long and narrow. Postgeneials small, separated by a scutum. Oculars 0–1. Rostral elevated, not separating internasals. Tail slender, 5.75 times in the total length. Gastrosteges 131, anal 1, urosteges 39. Color of body above and entire tail, black, a series of large distant red spots on each side, which often meet above, forming half-rings. These disappear on tail and neck. Below red, lower lip and chin black. Length 12–14 inches.

San José, Costa Rica. Dr. Van Patten.

This species differs from the *C. nasale*, Cope (Proceed. Academy, 1868, p. 131), in the fewer scale-rows (the latter has seventeen), the coloration, etc.

110. CATOSTOMA BRACHYCEPHALUM, Cope; *Colobognathus brachycephala*, Cope, loc. cit. 1871, p. 211.

Scales in fifteen longitudinal rows, smooth except a faint trace of carination near the posterior part of the body. Head flat, rather wide behind and distinct from neck. Postgeneials small, separated by a scale. Rostral moderate, internasals not minute, prefrontals nearly as broad as long. Frontal broad, convex in front, superciliary and parietal sutures nearly continuous. Oculars 0–1. Superior labials six, two behind orbit, sixth longer than high, separated by one temporal; fifth longer than high, bounding parietal; third and chiefly fourth in eye. Lower labials seven; gencials short, wide. Gastrosteges 124, anal 1, urosteges 38.

Color of body above and entire tail, black; gastrosteges reddish, brown margined. A yellowish or orange collar crosses behind the parietal plates and a band of the same color extends from the side of the neck to the tail on the second and third rows in front and third to fifth behind. This band is composed of two rows of alternating narrow spots, which are not always perfectly united.

Total length eight inches, the tail one-sixth of the total.

The species just described agree with the *C. nasale*, the *C. semidoliatum*, and the *Colobognathus hoffmannii*, in having the first labial behind the eye in contact with the parietal shield. They are intermediate in the structure of the jaws, between the types of the two genera named.   In the *C. semidoliatum* the maxillary bone is developed and bears teeth opposite the first labial plate.   In the *Colobognathus hoffmannii*, it with the palatine is cartilaginous in front, and bears no teeth anterior to the fourth labial shield.   In the *C. brachycephalum* and *C. dolichocephalum*, the maxillary and palatine are better developed, the teeth extending to the posterior margin of the second superior labial.   In the serpent described by me (Proc. Ac. Nat. Sci. 1869, p. 131) as *Cutostoma nasale*, the dentition is precisely as in the two species here described, while in the *C. bicolor*, Gthr., the character of the dentition is intermediate between them and that of the *C. semidoliatum*.   In the genus *Colophrys*, Cope, from Guatemala and Yucatan (l. c. 1868, p. 130), the maxillary is still better developed, the teeth commencing at the anterior part of the second upper labial.

111. COLODOGNATHUS HOFFMANNII, Peters, Monatsber. K. Preuss. Acad. 1863, p. 214.

PROTEROGLYPHA.

112. PELAMIS BICOLOR, Daudin.

This sea-snake has been now frequently brought from the Pacific coast of Central America since the first note of its occurrence there, Proceed. Academy Philadelphia, 1859, p. 347.

113. ELAPS MULTIFASCIATUS, Jan, Revue et Magazine Zoologie, 1859, Pl. A.   Cope, Proceed. Acad. Philada. 1871, p. 209.

San José ; Dr. Van Patten.

114. ELAPS ORNATISSIMUS, Jan, loc. cit.

San José ; Dr. Van Patten.

115. ELAPS NIGROCINCTUS, Girard, U. S. Astronomical Expedition, II. p. 210, plate.

San José ; Dr. Van Patten.

116. ELAPS CIRCINALIS, Dum. Bibron.

Several specimens with the rings varying in number from eleven to eighteen. Scales in the intervals black tipped.   Talamanca.

SOLENOGLYPHA.

TELEURASPIDES, Cope, Proceed. Academy Philada. 1871, p. 205.

This group of the rattlesnake family embraces those with undivided anal shields and no rattle.   It stands immediately between the true *Trigonocephali* and the *Crotali*, as the former have divided caudal scutella and the rattle absent, the latter possess the rattle with simple scutella.   One genus of this division was described long ago by Beauvois, and adopted by Gray and others, that is the *Ancistrodon* of North America and Mexico, but most of the genera have only been recognized within a recent period. In March, 1859, Prof. Peters distinguished a second genus of the group, and towards the close of the same year the writer named a third. Prof. Peters named another genus, which may be retained, though in a sense quite different from that in which it was originally intended. I allude to *Bothriopsis*, first defined by the four small scuta on the top of the muzzle of one of the species, a character not worthy of such a valuation. The characters adopted will be seen below. All the known species are found between north Mexico and Peru.

I. Head scaled above.
    a. Body compressed, tail prehensile (*arboreal*).
A series of horn-like scales above the eye, outside of the superciliary shield.

                                                       Teleuraspis.
Superciliary reaching to the edge of the eye opening; no horns.   *Bothriechis.*
    aa. Body cylindric, tail straight (*terrestrial*).
Nasal plate one.   *Porthidium.*
Nasal plates two.   *Bothriopsis.*
II. Head with nine plates above.
Body cylindric; two nasals.   *Ancistrodon.*

117. TELEURAPSIS SCHLEGELII, Berthold, Abh. Wiss. Göttingen, 1847, iii. 13 (*Trigonocephalus*). Cope, Pr. A. N. Sci. 1859, p. 338 ; 1860, p. 345.

This species is abundant in eastern Costa Rica, and displays three color varieties. All the specimens have twenty-three rows of scales, and some eight, and others nine superior labials. There is no tendency to division of the urosteges. From Ecuador to Costa Rica.

Var. I, *nitida*, Günther, Proc. Zool. Soc. Lond. 1859, nov. Tab. (*Lachesis*), l. c. 345, et 1868, p. 110.

Green with brownish-red vertical bands on each side which usually alternate ; belly green and yellow varied with black, punctulate. Ecuador.

Var. II. Green with a series of small brown dorsal spots; below as in Var. I.

Var. III, *nigroadspersus*, Steindachner, Sitzungsberg. Wien. Akademie, 1870, May, Pl. VIII.

Golden yellow ; lower surfaces unspotted.

According to the observation of Mr. Gabb, this is a dangerous species, its bite requiring prompt treatment to prevent a fatal result. It is distributed from the coast (Old Harbor) inland to an elevation of 5–600 feet above the sea.

38

118. BOTHRIECHIS NIGROVIRIDIS, Peters, l. c.; Cope, l. c.; Monatsber. K. Preuss. Akademie, 1859,
p. 278; Cope, Pr. A. N. Sci. Phila. 1859, p. 345; *Thamnocenchris*, Salvin.

This genus is, like the last, confined to the great forests of Central America
and the northwest of South America. Species have been found further north than
those of *Teleuraspis*. Like the latter they inhabit trees, filling the place in America
of the species of the East Indies which belong to the *Bothropes*, and of the tree-
vipers of Africa, *Atheris*, Cope. All the species of these different groups are of
green colors, in contradistinction to those of terrestrial habits, which are of various
shades of brown. This is evidently related to their convenience in the struggle
for existence in the localities in question.

From an elevated point on the Pico Blanco. Mr. Gabb states that it occurs
in the central valley also, from which it has been brought by Dr. Van Patten.

119. BOTHRIECHIS LATERALIS, Peters, Monatsb. K. Preuss. Acad. 1862, p. 674; *Bothrops bilinea-*
tus, Pet., l. c. 1859, p. 278; *? Bothrops bicolor*, Bocourt, Ann. des Sci. Nat. 1868, p. 201.
Costa Rica.

120. BOTHRIOPSIS AFFINIS, Bocourt, Ann. Sci. Nat. 1868, p 201; *Teleuraspis mexicanus*, Cope,
Pr. A. N. S. 1859, p. 339; *Bothriechis do.*, Cope, l. c. 1860, p. 345; nec *Atropus mexicanus*,
D. B.

Mexico, as far north as Tuxpan, and Central America to Costa Rica.

Superciliary shields very narrow; no small scales surrounding rostral. Scales
in 23 ("25") rows, three inferior smooth; small scales on canthus, four rows below
eye; rostral broad as high; nine superior labials, fourth largest. Twenty-two
dorsal rhombs.

The species of this genus are all of terrestrial habits, and approach in this
respect the *Ancistrodontes*. They have a more extended range than any of the
preceding, occurring from the upper or Peruvian Amazon to northern Mexico.
They are very venomous, but not so much dreaded as the true *Bothropes* of the
same regions, which attain a larger size.

121. BOTHRIOPSIS PROBOSCIDEUS, sp. nov.

A rather small species of sombre colors, allied to the *B. brachystoma*. Scales
in twenty-three series, all carinate, the inferior but slightly; those of the top of
the head and muzzle not very different in size, also keeled. Superciliary plates
each a broad oval, the two separated by five rows of scales, of which the external
on each side follows the inner border of the plate. A narrow shield on each side
of the end of the muzzle which is bent up at its middle, lying against the posterior
side of the rostral plate, and in contact with its fellow, the extremities of the two
having a bilobed outline. Rostral plate three times as high as wide, lying against

the plates just described by its upper part, the three forming an erect appendage or short proboscis. Nasal plates distinct, the posterior impressed, the anterior in the plane of the rostral, with an anterior angle produced between the rostral and superior plate of the muzzle. Pit surrounded by small scales; one large preocular. Labials nine above, fifth longest, separated from the orbit by three rows of scales. Lower labials nine, one pair of short gencials, followed by two pairs of shorter scales.

		M.
Total length	.	.310
Length of tail	.	.040
" to rictus oris	.	.015
Width of head at supercilia	.	.008
" " " temples	. .	.016

Color yellowish-brown above, blackish below. On the upper surface of the body eighteen quadrate spots divided by a narrow, light vertebral line, and divided in the transverse direction so that each is composed of four spots, which are smaller and most separated on the anterior part of the body. Lips black, the lower with vertical white bars. A brown band from eye to behind angle of mouth, bordered by white in front; a semidiscoid brown spot below eye.

This venomous snake resembles the *Porthidium nasutum* of Bacourt, according to the description of that author, but it is stated to have but one nasal shield, while all of the specimens of the *B. proboscideus* possess two.

Not rare at Sipurio, at the base of the mountains.

TRIGONOCEPHALI.

122. BOTHROPS ATROX, Linn.

Abundant in the coast region; one specimen measures six feet, and Mr. Gabb assures me that it reaches eight feet in length. It is the most formidable venomous snake in the country, and is known by the name of Tamagaf. Its bite is generally fatal, unless very promptly treated. Dr. C. R. Lordley, a resident in the country for many years, has saved many cases by the following treatment: He forbids alcohol, and administers fifteen drops of ammonia diluted every quarter or half hour, which, if not speedily beneficial, is replaced by the same amount of tincture of iodine. Salt is especially to be avoided, as well as fresh vegetable food, light animal diet being recommended. Hemorrhage into the stomach and alimentary canal is said to be aggravated by salt. The bowels are to be kept open by sufficient doses of castor oil. The usual violent thirst is not to be quenched by water, but by tea of cinnamon or guaca.

123. LACHESIS STENOPHRYS, Cope, sp. nov.

Scales in thirty-six longitudinal series, of which ten on each side of the median line support a central tubercle. The muzzle is short and depressed, and the rostral plate is an equilateral triangle. The superior labials number nine, of which the third is much the largest. The second is low, and does not bound the maxillary pit. The latter is bordered by three scuta; the superior narrow, bounds the two preoculars; the inferior wider, stands on the third labial, and the anterior, which is subcrescentic, and stands on the second superior labial. A trapezoid dorsal bounds the large superior preocular in front. Four rows of scales separate the orbit from the labials. The scales of the top of the head are flat, hexagonal, and faintly keeled; twelve series separate the superciliaries, which are quite narrow. Inferior labials thirteen, the first large, and with the second in contact with the geneials. The latter form but one pair, are squarely truncate in front, and narrowly rounded behind. Gastrosteges 200; urosteges, double 32, quadruple 17; caudal spine well developed. Color (in spirits) fawn brown, with twenty-three reddish-brown median rhombs on the dorsal region. The lateral angles of these are dark spots, sometimes isolated, and do not extend below the fifth row of scales. On the middle of the body the rhombs have pale centres, posteriorly they are darker, and become confluent into a zigzag band. Tail dark brown, with narrow, light cross bands. Lower surfaces all greenish-yellow, except the throat and chin, which are white (in spirits). A black band extends from the eye above the labials, and is broken upon the neck into a series of black spots. Top of head uniform brown.

				M.
Total length	.	.	.	.495
Length of tail	.	.	.	.050
" of gape	.	.	.	.021

One specimen from Sipurio.

This species is of much interest as increasing our knowledge of the structural and geographical range of the genus *Lachesis*, heretofore represented only by the *L. mutus* of Surinam. As such, it has the distal caudal scutella four-rowed and tubercular.

CROTALI.

124. CROTALUS DURISSUS, Linn.; *C. horridus*, Auctor., Phv.; *Caudisona durissa*, Laurenti.

This large species was not found by Dr. Gabb in Talamanca, but was brought by Dr. Van Patten from the neighborhood of San José.

TESTUDINATA.

125. SPHARGIS CORIACEA, Linn.

Young specimens from Limon, indicating a breeding place for this species.

126. CINOSTERNUM LEUCOSTOMUM, Dum.

Young and adults from Old Harbor and Sipurio.

127. CINOSTERNUM ALBOGULARE, Dum. Boc. Miss. Sci. Mexique, p. 24.

128. PSEUDEMYS ORNATA, Bell; *Callichelys ornata*, Gray, Supplem. Catal. Shield Reptiles, p. 48.

129. CHELOPUS GABBII, sp. nov.

Form resembling *Testudo*, stout, and with short thick feet with very short webs. Outline of carapace a regular ellipse, the margin not incised, but a little revolute behind and before. Top of shell flat in profile, bearing a well-marked but obtuse keel from nuchal plate to the caudals. Vertebral scuta (in an adult) broader than long, with straight transverse sutures; penultimate narrower behind, the last one the largest of all, wider than long. Plastron flat, turned up at the bridges and in front, strongly notched behind. The anterior lobe is concavely truncate in front, with a tooth-like protuberance at each outer angle; the sides oblique to the axilla. Gular scuta wide, their common suture not longer than that of the humerals.

Muzzle nearly vertical, beak not notched; symphysis recurved, horny alveolar ridge minutely serrate. Forearm with large scales in front, on the outer edge, and in a transverse band behind the wrist. Hind leg with a row of large scales on the inner front of the lower half of the tibia, continuous with those covering the inner toe. Two scales on the outer posterior border of the hind foot, followed by a large one covering the rudimental outer toe, which forms an obtuse process. Tail smooth.

Color above wood brown, middle of plastron from humeral scuta to posterior border darker brown; remainder of lower surfaces, wax-yellow. Head brown above, a faint red band round the muzzle, and a short one on the median line above. A yellowish brown-edged band from the temple to the middle of the neck, and a similar one from the eye to the tympanum. Neck and limbs yellowish, speckled with brown and black; hind legs blackish on the outer side.

		M.
Length of carapace		.186
Width of "		.120
Elevation of "		.060

This essentially terrestrial tortoise resembles the *C. areolatus*, Duméril, and the *C. annulatus* (*Rhinoclemmys*, Gray). The former has a roof-shaped back, and has

39

the vertebral scuta longer than wide. According to Gray, the keels of the vertebral scuta of the *C. annulatus* are confined to their anterior part, and the colors are materially different. It also resembles the *C. incisus*, Bocourt; but this turtle is represented as without the row of scuta on the inner front of the tibia ; the edge of the carapace is strongly dentate, and the gular scuta are much longer, and have a very different anterior margin. I only know this species from the figure and description of Bocourt.

The *Chelopus gabbii* is dedicated to the learned geologist who made the collection here described.

130. CHELOPUS FUNEREUS, sp. nov.

Represented by four specimens, none of which are adult, the largest having a carapace 4.75 inches in length. On examination with the view of ascertaining whether they represent the young of the *C. gabbii*, I find so many distinguishing features as to render it necessary to name them.

As in young tortoises, the carapace is wider than in adults of the same species. It is not revolute and very slightly serrate behind. An obtuse vertebral keel. Plastron notched behind ; the anterior lobe with a shallow concavity of the anterior border, the edge on each side of it projecting in three teeth. The free border of the humeral scute is strongly convex behind the gular. The feet are more strongly webbed in this species than in the last, and there are five scuta on the external border of the hind foot, which do not terminate in a large one, since there is no projection representing the outer toe. There is no row of scuta on the inner face of the tibia ; but the forearm is plated in front, on the outer edge, and in a band behind the wrist. In the smaller specimens there is a slight notch in the border of the upper jaw, in the larger it is absent. The median suture of the gular scuta is twice as long as that of the humerals. The first vertebral scute is relatively longer than the others, while the last one is only half as large as those that precede it.

Color black on the upper surface of the head, neck, and carapace ; plastron black, except a narrow, yellowish border. Throat, limbs, and marginal scuta below, yellowish, black speckled. Outer side of hind legs and feet, and outer edge of fore legs black. Some rows of black spots on the lower jaw and front of fore leg ; anterior toes yellow, with black borders No markings on the upper side of head and neck.

The adult of this species will probably be found to be of very obscure color. It displays unusual tardiness in the ossification of both carapace and plastron, the largest specimen being very soft. It is probably allied to the *Mauremys fuliginosa* of Gray. From Limon.

ART. V.—*On the Batrachia and Reptilia collected by Dr. John M. Bransford during the Nicaraguan Canal Survey of* 1874.

By E. D. COPE.

BATRACHIA.

1. CŒCILIA OCHROCEPHALA, Cope, Proceed. Academy Philada. 1866, 132.
   From the Atlantic side of the Isthmus.

2. MICROPHRYNE PUSTULOSA, Cope, Proceed. Academy Philada. 1864, 180.
   Buchio Soldado.

3. BUFO HÆMATITICUS, Cope, loc. cit., 1862, p. 157.
   Camp Mary Caretta.

4. BUFO PLEUROPTERUS, Schmidt, Denkschriften Wiener Academie, 18.
   Buhio Soldado and Camp Mary Caretta.

5. BUFO AGUA, Daudin.

6. HYLA ELÆOCHROA, Cope, Journal Philada. Academy, 1875, supra, p. 105.
   ? From the Pacific side.

7. PHYLLOBATES RIDENS, Cope, loc. cit., 1866, p. 131.

8. LITHODYTES DIASTEMA, Cope, sp. nov.

Approximating *Phyllobates* in the slight development of the vomerine teeth, and further characterized by the shortness of its feet. The former are in two very short transverse patches behind and within the line of the middle of the choanæ, and separated by an interspace as wide as the length of each. The tongue is obpyriform, rounded and extensively free behind. The *ostia pharyngea* are minute. The *membranum tympani* is indistinct, with a diameter of less than half that of the eye slit. The head is an oval in outline, with narrowly truncate and depressed muzzle. The canthus is obtuse, but not concave. Nares subterminal; diameter of orbit about equal length of head in front of it. Cranium above slightly convex in both directions.

The toes are short, and the digital dilations are large on all the feet. On the anterior the first toe is shorter than the second. On the posterior the fifth is longer than the third, and reaches the base of the penultimate phalange of the third. The muzzle marks the wrist and the middle of the tibia of the extended limbs.

(155)

Color above dark brown; a darker brown between the eyes, which is paler bordered anteriorly. Below, pale brown.

		M.
Total length .	.	.0200
Length to axilla .	.	.0090
" to tympanum .	.	.0060
Width head at tympanum	.	.0070
Length of fore limb	.	.0115
" of fore foot .	.	.0035
" of hind limb .	.	.0270
" of hind foot .	.	.0120
" of tibia	.	.0085
" of tarsus		.0060

This species resembles the *Lithodytes habenatus*, Cope (supra, p. 109), in the position of the vomerine teeth, but differs much in the form of the feet. In that frog the dilatations are much smaller and the feet much longer. In the hind foot this is chiefly due to the elongation of the fourth toe, which exceeds the third and fifth by three and a sixth phalanges.

The *Lithodytes diastema* was found by Dr. Bransford at the camp Mary Caretta, Panama.

LACERTILIA.

9. CORYTHOPHANES CRISTATUS, Merrem.

Buhio Soldado.

10. BASILISCUS GUTTULATUS, Cope, sp. nov.

Represented by a young male, which displays a number of remarkable characters. The back and median line of the tail support the membranous crest stretched between the elongate neural spines as seen in *B. plumifrons*, *B. mitratus*, etc., but the head-crest, instead of being covered, as in those species with large thin scales, presents only small smooth scales like those of the occipital region. This crest is also of smaller size than in the species named, only beginning to rise from a line connecting the tympanic drums, although preceded by a keel to near the line of the border of the orbits. It is not much elevated, but is prolonged chiefly backwards, and has a truncate posterior outline. Points in which the species differs from the *B. cristatus* are, the presence of two large scuta bounding the rostral shield above, and the presence of two large labials behind the point of junction with the suborbital ring of scales. There are only ten rays to the dorsal fin, and fifteen to the caudal, the latter graduating imperceptibly to the usual keel. Neither crest is bordered at the margin with large scales. The ventral scales are entirely smooth, while the dorsals are smaller and keeled; the lateral are smaller still.

Color olivaceous-brown above, shaded with leaden on the sides; yellowish below. A few black spots at the base of the dorsal crest. Sides and throat with small black spots. A black band from eye to tympanum, bordered with yellow below. Hind legs and feet with brown, yellow-bordered cross-bands.

	M.
Total length	.455
Length to vent	.125
" to axilla .	.060
" to tympanum .	.030
" to orbit . .	.012
Width between orbits	.016
Length of fore limb	.060
" of hind limb .	.130
" of hind foot .	.063

From camp at Buhio Soldado, Panama.

11. ANOLIS TROCHILUS, Cope, Proceed. Academy Philada., 1871, p. 215.
Buhio Soldado.

12. ANOLIS PETERSII, Bocourt, Miss. Scient. Mexique, p. 79.
Station 19.

13. ANOLIS CAPITO, Peters.
Rio Frijole.

14. AMIVA PRÆSIGNIS, Bd. Gird.

OPHIDIA.

15. SPILOTES CORAIS, L.; subspecies MELANURUS, Dum. Bibr.

16. XENODON ANGUSTIROSTRIS, Peters.
Camp Mary Caretta.

17. SIBON ANNULATUM, Linn.
From the Atlantic side.

18. TELEURASPIS SCHLEGELII, Berth.
From the Atlantic side.

Total number of species obtained by Dr. Bransford, eighteen.

Art. VI.—*Report on the Reptiles brought by Professor James Orton from the middle and upper Amazon, and western Peru.*

By E. D. Cope.

THE following pages contain a list of the species as expressed in the above title, including descriptions of such as have not been previously known to zoology. A report on the Batrachia obtained by Prof. Orton has already appeared,* which included thirty-six species; of these fourteen were believed to be new. The present list embraces seventy-four species, of which seventeen are new. The *Lacertilia* number thirty-three species, the *Ophidia* forty-one.

The localities at which the greater number of species were obtained are: Santarem (on the lower Amazon); Solimoens (or middle Amazon); the Marañon (or upper Amazon) at several points, viz., near the mouth of the Napo, at Iquitos and Nauta on the Peruvian and Ecuadorian borders; on the Huallaga between Balsa Puerto and Moyabama, and near Moyabamba and Rioja, Peru. A few specimens were obtained near Lake Titicaca, which represent three species, viz.: *Cyclorhamphus œmaricus*, Cope; *Tachymenis chilensis*, Schlegel; and *Proctotretus multiformis*, Cope. These all belong to genera of the Pacific side of the Andes, none of which are known from east of that range, and the *Tachymenis chilensis* is the commonest snake of Chili and western Bolivia. The indications respecting the fauna of eastern Peru furnished by Professor Orton's collections are, that it differs in no essential respect from that of the great Amazon valley.

The Peruvian species were mostly derived from the valley of Jequetepeque, which extends from the Cordillera of Caxamarca to near the coast at Pacasmayo. They are sixteen in number, and include type forms of the West Coast Fauna in the genera *Microlophus* and *Craniopeltis*.

LACERTILIA.

LEPTOGLOSSA.

1. MABUIA CEPEDEI, Gray; Cope, Proceed. Academy Philada. 1862, p. 186.
   Nauta.

2. MABUIA SURINAMENSIS, Hallowell, Cope, loc. cit.
   From the Marañon near the mouth of the Napo.

* Proceedings Academy Philada., 1874, p. 120.

3. Propus vermiformis, Cope, Proceed. Acad. Philada. 1874, p. 70.

From Nauta.

4. Lepidosoma carinicaudatum, Cope, sp. nov.

Scales large, angulate, strongly keeled on the back and sides; four abdominal rows with the keel reduced to an angle and mucro, otherwise like the dorsal scales. The dorsals are a little larger than the ventrals, and these a little larger than the inferior lateral. A few small scales in the groin and axilla, and above the humerus. No granular scales on the side of the neck, but keeled scales between the arm and ear. Nuchal scales like the dorsal; the gulars a little smaller than the ventrals, keeled and mucronate. Four superior rows of caudal scales strongly keeled, forming four continuous ridges. Two lateral rows weakly keeled; four inferior series strongly keeled, forming ridges. Twenty-six oblique rows of scales between occiput and posterior line of femora; twenty-seven between infralabials and femoral pores, and twenty-one in a circle round the body. Two large preanal scuta, each flanked by a small lateral, and preceded by an oval median scale, which has a small one on each side.

The frontonasal plate is broader than long; the prefrontals not extensively in contact, and the frontal is twice as long as wide. The frontoparietals are largely in contact, and the parietals and interparietals are longitudinal and subequal in size. Two loreals, one above the other, no preoculars; five supraoculars and four supraorbitals. The temporal scales small, smooth; larger and keeled behind. Cranial plates behind the prefrontals with one or two linear ridges. Three pairs of very large infralabials, a row of granules only separating ths last pair. Eleven femoral pores on each side. The diameter of the oval meatus auditorius is equal to that of the eye-slit. The limbs are covered with large keeled scales, except the postero-inferior faces of the femur and humerus, which are granulated. The limbs are short, the anterior reaching the middle of the orbit, the posterior five-sixths the distance to the axilla. Thumb clawed.

		M.
Total length (tail partly renewed)	.	.115
Length to vent . . .	.	.050
" to axilla . .	.	.021
" to ear . .	.	.011
" to orbit . . .		.003
Width of head at angle of jaws .	.	.0085
Length of hind limb . .	.	.023
" of hind foot .		.011

Color above cinnamon-brown, below yellow; sides, from ear to an indefinite point on the tail, black, inclosing a narrow yellow band from axilla to groin. Black on scapular region, pale bordered above. From nape to tail a median series of small black spots. Head brown; throat yellow.

This handsome species differs from the *L. scincoides* of Spix in the absence of a band of granular scales on the sides of the neck, and in the keeled scales of the tail. The coloration is quite distinct. It differs in many specific details from the *Loxopholis rugiceps*, Cope,* besides in the quadrate form of the abdominal scuta, in which that genus differs from *Lepidosoma*.

From the Maranon.

5. Neusticurus ecpleopus, Cope, sp. nov.

Scales of the back small and flat, becoming granular on the nape. Mingled with the former are large oval keeled scales in two separate rather irregular series near the middle, and a double row of similar ones on each side. The sides are thrown into vertical folds, which support mingled small and large scales. The nape and sides of the neck are marked by rows of small round warts, of which there are eight between the lines of the tympana.

The abdominal scales are in eight longitudinal rows, the median as broad as long, except at the sides. There is a well-marked collar of seven scales, large in the middle and small exteriorly. In front of this are four or five cross series of large scales, all but the posterior composed of two scales only. The throat is otherwise covered with round, smooth, convex scales. The preanal region is covered with three rows of scales, the anterior two containing two each, the last or marginal including two large, and a small median one. The limbs above are granular, with scattered tubercles; femur and forearm in front, and tibia below, with large scuta. Tail, with whorls of oblong scales with two keeled rows above, which are separated by a few flat scales only.

The head scuta are the usual ones, with the omission of internasals. The parietals are about as large as the frontoparietals, and are separated by a larger interparietal, which projects further backwards, forming with the parietals a nearly rectangular outline, the angle median. Four infraorbitals, five supraoculars. A loreal and upper preocular, which cover part of canthus rostralis. Temporal scales granular. Upper labials seven, four to the coronoid process, large, especially the fourth; fifth subtriangular. Inferior labials four and five to coronoid, of which some two are confluent in the typical specimen. A large postsymphyseal; four

---

* Proceed. Academy Phila. 1868, 305.

large infralabials, of which three are in contact with the labials, and two pairs with each other. Ear as large as eye opening. Femoral pores fifteen on each side.

Color chocolate-brown above, showing darker spots in proper lights; below yellow, brown speckled, except the throat and chin and lips, which are black.

		M.
Length (tail partly reproduced)	.	.130
" to vent . .		.066
" to axilla .		.033
" to tympanum .	.	.015
" to orbit . . .	.	.005
Width of head behind . . .	. .	.012
Length of fore limb	. .	.020
" of hind limb	. .	.030
" of hind foot	. .	.015

The characters which distinguish this species from the long-known and large *N. bicarinatus*, are the larger gular scuta, the smaller occipital and temporal scales, the eight (not six) ventral rows, and the fifteen (not thirty) femoral pores.

The characters of the head scuta of this genus are those of the *Ecpleopidæ*; while those of *Thorictis* and *Crocodilurus* are those of the *Teidæ*.

6. CROCODILURUS AMAZONICUS, Spix.

7. CENTROPYX PELVICEPS, Cope, Proceed. Academy Philada. 1868, 98.

Nauta.

8. CENTROPYX DECODON, Cope, loc. cit., 1861, 495.

Santarem, Brazil.

9. CENTROPYX ALTAMAZONICUS, Cope, sp. nov.

Dorsal scales very small, hexagonal, smooth, but little larger than the lateral. Ventrals keeled, in sixteen longitudinal rows, and thirty-five transverse to the line of the femoral pores. Two rows of keeled collar scales, the second largest. Gular scales small, equal, and smooth. Four rows of carinate preanal scales, the last composed of six scales.

Internasal scuta barely attaining mutual contact; frontonasal broader than long; mutual contact of prefrontals short. Frontal longer than wide, parietals nearly as wide as interparietal (the specimen young). Two narrow transverse occipitals. Nostril on suture between internasal and nasal; one large loreal, one inferior preocular; six supraoculars, and three supraorbitals. Scuta on the upper and front sides of humerus, and front of cubitus; other faces granular. Femur and tibia granular above, the former behind also. Inferior tibial scuta keeled. Caudal scuta keeled below, nearly and quite smooth above.

Color of a young specimen bluish, with a median light band from the middle of the back to the end of the nose, covering the muzzle and front as far as the frontoparietal scuta. A light band from orbit to near femur and another from tympanum to groin, the intervening space crossed by vertical black spots and bars. Lower surfaces green immaculate.

		M.
Total length	.	.110
Length to vent	.	.040
" to axilla . . .	.	.019
" to ear	.	.010
" to orbit	.	.004
Width of head posteriorly . .	. .	.006
Length of hind limb . .	. . .	.029
" of hind foot .	. . . . .	.015

This species is nearer to the *C. calcaratus* than to the *C. decodon*, but differs from it in the more numerous ventral scales, keeled preanals, less numerous femoral pores, etc. From Moyabamba, Peru.

10. DICRODON OALLISCELIS, Cope, sp. nov.

The inner cusp of each tooth smaller than the outer. Nostril in the internasal plate close to the posterior and inferior suture. Scales of the belly large, transverse, smooth, in eight rows; those of the back commencing as granulations on the interscapular region, and gradually increasing in size until they are similar in size to the large ones which cover the tail in whorls. Like the latter they are keeled, the keels forming continuous lines. There are thirteen series at the groin, and eighteen one-third the length behind the axillæ. Nuchal scales and those of the sides of the neck and body granular. Posterior face of humerus, postero-superior faces of cubitus, superior and posterior faces of femur, and superior face of tibia granular; other faces of limbs scutate. Femoral pores eighteen on each side. Anal scuta in three longitudinal series of alternating rhombic plates. Margin of neck fold granular; its middle with five transverse rows of unequal transverse scales.

Internasals and prefrontals in extensive contact; the frontonasal hexagonal, longer than broad. Frontal narrow behind, angulate in front, divided transversely by a suture at the penultimate supraorbital scute. Frontoparietals very small, separated by the small interparietal which is in contact with the frontal. Two small suboval parietals on each side, and ten or twelve large scales surrounding them behind. Loreal elongate; labials 5–5. Four supraorbitals, the last two separated from the frontal by granules. Six large infralabials, the last three smaller and separated by two plates from the labials; the anterior pair in contact. Gular scales small, smooth, a wide band of smaller scales separating them from those of the collar.

		M.
Total length	.	.343
Length to vent	.	.099
"　　to axilla	.	.040
"　　to ear	.	.022
"　　to orbit . .	.	.011
Width of head behind		.014
Length of hind limb	.	.073
"　　of hind foot	.	.037

Color olive above, becoming yellow posteriorly and on the tail; below yellowish-olive. A dark line bounding the dorsal scales on the side, and a row of small blackish spots along the middle of the granular lateral band. Femur yellow behind, with two parallel black bands. Tail with light bluish spots on the sides. Head, back, and belly unicolor.

This fine and very distinct species was brought by Prof. Orton from Pacasmayo, on the Pacific coast of northern Peru.

11. CNEMIDOPHORUS LEMNISCATUS, Daudin. Duméril, Bibron, V. p. 128.

From the Marañon and the Amazonas at Santarem.

12. CNEMIDOPHORUS ARMATULUS, sp. nov.

Tongue not furcate behind, but not received into a sheath as in *Amiva*. Abdominal scales smooth in eight longitudinal rows; preanal scuta in three rows of two each, followed by two small round scuta in longitudinal line, surrounded by small scales except in front. On each side of these a group of five spur-shaped scales, with projecting acute apices, in two rows, of which the posterior includes three. Gular fold bordered with small scales, which are preceded by two cross-rows of large scutella. Gular region with a few median scutella of the same size which graduate into those surrounding.

Head rather elongate, frontal not divided; frontoparietals distinct, longer than wide. Three supraorbitals, the anterior partly isolated. Parietals and interparietals each longer than wide, surrounded on the sides and behind by one series of flat scales much larger than those of the nape. The latter, with those of the back and sides, subequal, flat, subhexagonal, and of small size. Scuta of front and back of humerus continuous with each other, and nearly so with those of cubitus, which form two rows, the posterior very wide. Femoral pores twelve. The fore foot reaches the nostril; the posterior, the middle of the tympanum.

Color bright olive-green, with yellow muzzle, and a pale dorsal band. There are three pale lines on the side, from the orbit, ear, and axilla respectively, of which the middle one is interrupted and separated from the superior by an irregular black band. Below white, sides blue. Length from end of muzzle to vent, m. .048.

From the valley of Jequetepeque, Peru.

This species resembles the *Amiva hedracantha*, Boc., Miss. Scient. Mexique, p. 263, in its preanal spines and other respects. According to M. Bocourt that species has but one frontoparietal shield, which is of unusually short proportions, thus resembling the genus *Verticaria*, Cope. It also differs from the *C. armatulus* in the presence of two preoculars (one in *C. armatulus*), and in having a single large median preanal plate.

13. AMIVA SURINAMENSIS, Gray, Dum. Bibr. Erp. Gen., V. p. 100.

Rioja and Nauta, Peru; Marañon, and Santarem.

IGUANIA.

14. SCYTOMYCTERUS LÆVIS, Cope, gen. et sp. nov. Anolidarum.

Char. Gen.—General structure as in *Anolis*, the posterior teeth with three cusps, the median larger. Rostral plate produced into a flexible appendage.

This form approaches nearest to the *Anolis gracilis*, in which the end of the muzzle is slightly protuberant, but is not prolonged into a process. This species has been erected into a genus by Dr. Gray under the name of *Rhinosaurus*, without, as it appears to me, sufficient reason. The name is also preoccupied.

Char. Specif.—Scales of the body smooth, of nearly equal size; those of the tail larger, the median superior series not different from the others. Scales of the head large and smooth, only three rows between those of the canthus rostralis at the middle. The latter are unusually wide, and the median row larger than those on each side of it. The latter are continued posteriorly into the superciliary rows, which are large, and in contact along the entire middle line. The middle row of the muzzle is replaced by two rows in the shallow frontal concavity. There are four rows between the nostrils. The occipital is large, in contact with superciliary shields in front, and with flat scales behind. One row of loreal scales, except at the orbit, where there are two. Postocular and temporal scales equal to or larger than the dorsal. A series of large infralabials in contact with the labials throughout. Auricle half the size of the eye-slit. The legs are short; the fore foot only reaching to the front of the orbit, and the hind limb falling considerably short of the axilla. Toe expansions rather narrow. Lateral occipital crests prominent.

Color above dark gray, below pigmented white (in spirits). The two colors are abruptly defined between the orbit and the scapula, and there are brown spots behind the axilla. Tail distantly annulate.

	M.
Total length	.139
Length to vent .	.060
" to axilla	.027
" to meatus .	.017
" to orbit . .	.009
Width of head behind	.009
Length of fore limb .	.018
" of hind "	.027
" of hind foot	.012
" of tibia .	.007

From between Moyabamba and Balsa Puerto, on the river Huallaga in Eastern Peru.

Besides its generic characters, this species has larger head scales than the *A. gracilis*, where the superciliaries are separated by two series. The legs are shorter.

15. ANOLIS TRANSVERSALIS, Duméril, Archives du Museum, 1856, p. 515.

From Nauta.

Mr. O'Shaughnessy has recently (Annals Magaz. Nat. Hist. 1875) regarded the *A. impetigosus*, Cope, as identical with the present species. I think that it will be found on examination of the type specimen now in the British Museum, to differ from the *A. transversalis* in its larger abdominal scales, larger and fewer supraorbitals, less numerous large inferior caudals, and strikingly in the coloration.

A few other determinations of Mr. O'Shaughnessy's paper will require revision. Thus the specimen in the British Museum labelled *Chamaeleolis porcus* is not the species described by me under that name; the only specimen of it known to me, is in the museum of the Philadelphia Academy. *Anolis argenteolus* and *A. lucius* are distinct. The *A. chlorocyaneus*, of Dum. Bibr., includes two species, as their description indicates, and as I discovered by an examination of the type specimens in the museum of the Jardin des Plantes. One of these is the *A. cœlestinus*, Cope; for the other the name *A. chlorocyaneus* must be retained. Both *A. pentaprion* and *A. vittigerus* are abundantly distinct from the familiar *A. biporcatus* of Mexico; and *A. bitectus* and *A. ordinatus* are, I think, outside the range of variation of the species to which Mr. O'Shaughnessy refers them, though nearly allied. *Anolis spectrum*, Pet., is distinct from *A. cyanopleurus*, Cope.

16. ANOLIS ORTONII, Cope, Proceed. Acad. Philada. 1868, p. 97.

From Nauta. One of the specimens is brilliant golden, with green reflections.

17. ANOLIS BOCOURTII, Cope, sp. nov.

Allied to the preceding, and to the *A. trochilus* and *A. bransfordii*, Cope. The abdominal scales are small, flat, and smooth; the dorsals are smaller and thickened, but not keeled, and the laterals are a little smaller still, and subgranular. They graduate into the dorsals and ventrals. The tail is slightly compressed, but has no median keel. The head is elongate, exceeding the length of the tibia; the muzzle is longer than it is wide at the anterior margin of the orbits. Occipital scute small, a little exceeding the auricular meatus, and separated from the superciliaries by numerous flat scales. The superciliary scales separated by two or three rows of small scales. The facial rugæ are very obtuse, and are separated by a shallow concavity. The latter is floored with smooth scales, which are much smaller than those of the rugæ, a transverse line crossing eight of them. The scales of the front of the muzzle are larger, and twelve rows without keels may be counted between the canthal series. Supraorbitals few, surrounded by granules; consisting of one hexagonal smooth plate, surrounded, except on the inner side, by five similar or smaller ones. Seven loreal rows; labials 8–9; infralabials subequal, small, smooth, and in four rows. Auricular meatus half the size of the eye-slit. Fan large. The fore limb reaches the end of the muzzle, but the hind limb only reaches the front of the orbit.

		M.
Total length	.	. .1350
Length to vent		. .0450
" to axilla		. .0200
" to ear	.	. .0110
" to orbit	.	.0055
Width of head behind		.0060
Length of hind limb	.	.0335
" of hind foot	.	. .0145

Coppery-brown above ; below, light coppery, frequently dusted and speckled with brown, especially in females.

As compared with *A. bransfordii* and other allies, the *A. bocourtii* has a longer head, fewer and smooth supraorbital scales, and shorter hind legs. It is abundant at Nauta. I dedicate it to Dr. Bocourt of Paris, whose magnificent work on the Reptiles of Mexico has added much to our knowledge of the *Anolidæ*.

18. ANOLIS TRACHYDERMA, Cope, sp. nov.

Abdominal scales small, obtusely keeled ; three or four median dorsal series, nearly as large as the ventrals, flat, keeled, and quickly graduating into the granular scales of the sides. These, with the scales of neck, throat, and sides of the head, are angulate or subround so as to produce a shagreened surface. Tail round, curved with flat keeled scales. Occipital oval, small, nearly equal to ear, separated by two rows of elongate keeled scales. Facial rugæ obsolete, the scales on its usual position and external to it, larger than those that occupy the frontal concavity, which are narrow, keeled, and in five or six rows, arranged (in the only specimen) concentrically posterior to a median scale. Twelve rows at the middle of the muzzle, all flat and carinate. Supraorbitals keeled, arranged in a circle round two central scales, ten altogether. Six rows at middle of lores. Auricular meatus one-third of eye. Labials 9–11 ; infralabials not distinct from gulars, keeled.

Head oval, as long as tibia ; muzzle longer than wide at front of orbits. The fore limb reaches the end of the muzzle, but the hind limb only extends to the middle of the orbits. Fan large.

Color black, above and below, excepting thorax, abdomen, and inferior middle line of tail, which are fulvous. An indistinct light band across the chin, half way between eye and nostril.

	M.
Length of head and body	.055
" to axilla	.027
" to ear	.019
" to orbit	.006
Width of head behind	.008
Length of hind limb	.045
" of hind foot	.018

One female specimen from Nauta.

19. ANOLIS BOMBICEPS, Cope, sp. nov.

Abdominal scales keeled ; dorsals much smaller, smooth, and a little larger than the almost granular laterals. Tail subround, with equal scales. The head is short, wide, and convex above, with very large orbits. Its length to ear is less than that of the tibia, and the length of the muzzle less than the width at the front of the orbits. Occipital scute subround, larger than tympanum, surrounded by numerous smaller smooth scales. Superciliaries separated by two rows of small scuta. Rugæ distinct, low, inclosing a concavity containing smaller scales than the rugal, in four longitudinal rows. Ten rows crossed by a section of the muzzle at the middle. Supraorbitals seventeen or eighteen, smooth or nearly so. Lorcals six rows; infralabials scarcely distinct, keeled. Meatus round, equal half diameter of eye-slit. Fan small. The hind limb reaches beyond the front of the orbit, and the fore limb to beyond the end of the muzzle.

		M.
Total length .		. .1300
Length to vent .		. .0460
" to axilla .		. .0230
" to ear .		. .0118
" to orbit . .		. .0040
Width of head at jaws		. .0065
Length of hind limb .	.	. . .0400
" of hind foot .	.	. . .0170

General color bright olive, shaded with brown above. A dark band from ear to shoulder, and vertical blackish bars on the sides. Fan dark ? indigo. A longitudinal black band on the former behind. A white spot on each side of the lower jaw in three specimens.

Four specimens from Nauta.

This species is near the *A. trachydermus* and *A. lemurinus*, Cope. From the former, the very different form of head, the distinct rugal scales of the front, inclosing larger and smoother scales, with the small smooth dorsal scales distinguish it. The *A. lemurinus* resembles it in form, but has larger dorsal scales.

20. Nonors DUODECIMSTRIATUS, Berthold; *N. macrodactylus*, Hallow.

Two specimens from Santarem, Brazil.

21. IGUANA TUBERCULATA, Laur.

22. ENYALIUS LATICEPS, Guichenot in Castlenau's Anim. Nouv. ou rare Amer. Sud, pl.

23. ENYALIUS COERULESCENS, Cope, sp. nov.

A dentellated nuchal crest, a vertebral band of linear scales; no caudal crest; all subround in section. Head wide, the muzzle parabolic, its entire surface including the supraorbital region covered with equal, acutely tubercular scales. Three rows intervene between the superciliary rows ; occipital scarcely distinct. Nostril pierced in a small round shield ; nearer orbit than end of muzzle. Loreal region very short, with ten scales on a vertical line. Supraocular scales eighteen, counting to nostril. Labials 11–11, a short series of distinct, smooth infralabials. Auricular opening large. Dorsal scales very small, keeled, in transverse rows ; abdominal scales larger, in cross series, interrupted on the middle line, keeled. The hind leg and wrist extend to front of orbit.

Color black, with numerous indistinct blue cross bands. Limbs, especially the forearm, and the sides of the neck, dark blue. Lower surfaces white, except throat and chin, which are blackish-blue.

								M.
Total length	.							.185
Length to vent	.	.						.072
" to axilla	.	.			.	.	.	.034
" to ear	.	.	.			.	.	.018
" to orbit	.	.	.	.		.	.	.	.006

Width at anterior angle of orbit .009 ; apparently allied to the *E. brasiliensis*, Lesson (Voyage Coquille Reptiles, Pl. I., fig. 3), but that species has a dorsal crest of erect scales.

24. HYPERANODON OCHROCOLLARIS, Spix, Dum. Bibr. Erpet. Gen., V.

25. HYPERANODON PELTIGERUS, Cope, sp. nov.

Scales of belly, sides, and back of about equal size, the former keeled, those of sides and back without median keel, but with a strong mucro (the epidermis is lost). A crest of processes on the nape which extend on the back to its middle only as a row of keeled scales. Top of head covered with large scales ; the occipital broader than long, bounded behind by small scales and at the middle on each side by a small oval parietal. Three scales on the front between the canthus rostrales, the outer ones the front of the superciliary series, which are partially united between the orbits. Six scales across the front behind the nostrils. Supraorbitals in a single row of four transverse scales, which are bounded by a series of small ones on the inner border, and from one to two rows on the outer margin. Rostral narrow, horizontal ; four upper, five lower labials. Symphyseal deeper than wide, truncate behind ; one anterior infralabial larger than the rest, smooth. Scales of the limbs smooth, except a few with obsolete keels on the upper side of the humerus and of the femur. Cervical dermal fold strong, extending to a point above the humerus. Tympanum large ; nostril in a single plate, which is separated from the rostral and superior labial by a single row of scales. When the limbs are extended, the wrist reaches nearly to the end of the muzzle, and the longer toe to the posterior border of the orbits.

Color dark yellowish-brown above, light brown below. Nine dark cross bands on back between scapulæ and rump. A black spot in front of the scapula, with a pale shade above it. Head plates brown, with blue reflections. Tail annulate with brown.

				M.
Total length	.	.	.	.275
Length to vent	.	.	.	.087
" to axilla	.		.	.037
" to orbit	.	.	.	.008
Width of head behind		.	.	.019
Length of hind limb	.	. .	.	.067
" of hind foot	.	. . .	.	.028

This species differs materially from the last in its larger head-scuta, especially the supraorbitals, and smooth abdominal scales.

26. Doryphorus flaviceps, Guichenot in Castlenau's Voyage in Amér. Meridionale.

27. Hypsibates agamoides, Wiegmann, Dum. Bibr.

From Moyabamba, Peru.

28. Microlophus heterolepis, Wiegmann; *Tropidurus heterolepis*, Wiegm. Nova Acta Caes. Leopold. Nat. Cur., xvii. p. 223, tab. 16.

Scales granular, a series forming a low crest from the nape to the end of the tail. No femoral nor anal pores. Tail compressed. Head with a broad interparietal shield, and large supraorbitals. Ear distinct; nostril above canthus rostralis. Two prehumeral folds, which nearly meet in the middle.

Abdominal scales much larger than the others, smooth, in transverse rows; those of the tail of equal size, half keeled. Nine smooth scales in a line across the middle of the muzzle. Nostrils subvertical in one plate, which is separated from the rostral by one scale, from its mate and from the labials by two scales. Superciliary rows in contact; interparietal broader than long. Five transverse smooth supraorbital scuta bordered within by one, and without by two rows of small scales, with a few of intermediate size between them and the latter. One very long suborbital; eyelids fringed with narrowly conic scales. Four loreal rows. Labial scales 7–7 to the coronoid elevation of the lower jaw, very narrow; the rostral broad, angulate above. Three large smooth infralabials separated from the inferior labials by small scales. Some weak dermal folds on the side of the neck, and two similar to them along each side. A strong vertical fold in front of each shoulder.

		M.
Total length (tail reproduced at end) .	.	.175
Length to vent	.	.070
" to axilla . . .	.	.032
" to meatus of ear . .	.	.015
Width of head behind . .	.	.013
Length of hind limb . . .	.	.047
" of hind foot . . .	. . . .	.021

The ear is partially closed in front by a narrow flap of skin, which supports several flat, acuminate, dermal denticles, of which two are most prominent. The limbs are rather short, the fore limb reaching the end of the muzzle, the hind limb not quite reaching the ear.

Color above light grayish-brown, with about eleven transverse series of small brown spots. Back also with distant yellow speckles; head light and dark brown speckled. Under surfaces yellowish-white, except the thoracic amfugular regions, which are black.

29. MICROLOPHUS INGUINALIS, sp. nov.; *Microlophus lessonii*, Var. Dum. Bibron, Erp. Gen., iv. p. 341.

Dorsal scales small, flat, a median larger row, scarcely elevated on the nape and tail, flat on the back. Two lateral folds from tympanum to groin; a prehumeral fold nearly meeting its mate on the thorax; a series of four or five denticulations in front of the ear. Parietal shield large, broader than long, Two rows of frontals (superciliaries), which unite on top of the muzzle in a circular rosette of seven smooth shields inclosing a small one in the centre. Four rows of scales between the nasal plates. One row of large, and one or two rows of small loreal scales. Four or five rows of infralabials, the gulars abruptly distinguished from them, and considerably smaller. The end of the external digit of the fore limb reaches the end of the muzzle, and the longest hinder toe reaches the nostril.

		M.
Length (tail entire)	.	. .151
" to vent .	. .	. .057
" to axilla .		. .025
" to ear . . .		. .013
" to orbit . . .		. .005
Width of the head behind		. .011

Emerald-green above, white below; a lateral black band which incloses at the groin a large longitudinal yellow spot. Limbs faintly yellow spotted. Throat with blue chevrons from the lips.

This species agrees with the *M. heterolepis* in many respects, although very distinct in coloration. It differs in squamation in the fewer loreals and more numerous muzzle scales. In *M. heterolepis*, the gular scales are scarcely smaller than the labials, and graduate regularly into them.

Valley of Jequetepeque, Peru.

30. MICROLOPHUS PERUVIANUS, Less.; *M. lessonii*, Dum. Bibr.

In this species there are four rows of scales between the nasal scales, and the infralabials and gulars are distinguished abruptly. It differs from the other species here described in the form of the parietal, which is longer than broad, as represented by Lesson (Voyage of the Coquille).

31. CRANIOPELTIS OCCIPITALIS, Bocourt; *Aneuporus occipitalis*, Bocourt; Mission Scientifique de Mexique, p. 215.

One specimen from Jequetepeque differs in coloration from that described by M. Bocourt, but not otherwise. It has a broad, brown dorsal band, which is crossed at rather remote intervals by deep brown, narrow cross-bars. Lower surfaces uniform white. *Aneuporus*, Boc., must yield to the prior *Craniopeltis*, Pet.

32. PROCTOTRETUS MULTIFORMIS, Cope, sp. nov.

Nostrils entirely above the canthus rostralis, laterosuperior in direction. External meatus of ear much larger than eye opening, its anterior border simple. Frontal plate subdivided, the middle portion not divided lengthwise. Three flat scales on front between canthus rostrales; interparietal small, in contact with superciliaries, and two occipitals of equal size behind it. Four entire, and one divided transverse supraorbitals. Labials $\frac{8}{6}$; four or five large infralabials, separated from labials by one row of scales in front and two behind. An irregular dermal fold extending posterior to the ear. Scales of side of neck, and scapular and axillary regions, granular. Those of back and sides of body rather small, flat, the dorsals weakly keeled, with smooth ones intermixed, the laterals nicked. Those of the lower surfaces a little larger, not notched. Scales of femur behind, small, flat, of lower side of humerus, granular; other scales of limbs like the dorsal, on the tibia, keeled. The fore foot reaches the nostril, and the hind foot the axilla. The dimensions of the largest specimen (var. 1) are as follows:—

44

	M.
Total length . .	. .190
Length to vent . .	. .093
" to axilla .	. .039
" to ear . .	. .023
" to orbit . .	. .008
" of hind limb .	. .052
" of hind foot .	. .023
Width of head behind	. .021

This species varies considerably in coloration, presenting the following varieties:—

I. Bright green, paler posteriorly, with two rows of large transverse black bars with irregular edges. Head brown above, pale speckled, lower surfaces olive. One specimen.

II. Olive-brown above, with faint darker cross-bands, pale bordered behind; sides and below blue to whitish; three specimens.

III. Light brown with a row of black spots on each side, divided by a longitudinal pale band. Below yellowish, marbled with bluish; one specimen.

All the specimens are from the elevated Lake of Titicaca, Peru.

NYCTISAURA.

33. PHYLLODACTYLUS INÆQUALIS, Cope, sp. nov.

Scales of back and sides subequal, the former of unequal sizes, but without elevated or keeled tubercles. Ventral scales larger, subround, smooth; those bordering the vent in front smaller. Muzzle with convex scales larger than those on the occiput. Labials to below the pupil, six above; below five, followed by three others; the inferior first three are the larger. Mental scutum longer than wide, angulate behind, with an oval scute on each side of the angle, which meet by an angle each on the middle line. Behind these are round scales from which others graduate into the granules of the throat. Meatus auditorius a very small slit. Eye contained nearly twice in length of muzzle. The fore limbs extended reach the front of the orbit; the hind limbs extend to the appressed elbow. Scales of the normal tail square, and flat above; rounded and a little larger below.

Above yellowish, with seven blackish cross-bands from nape to groin, somewhat connected by oblique and longitudinal lines on the sides. A dark band from nostril through eye to shoulder. Limbs and tail cross-banded. Head with a coarse, blackish reticulation above. A brown spot on each labial. Below straw-color, immaculate.

				M.
Length to vent	.		. .	.0380
" to axilla	.		. .	.0180
" to ear . .	.		. .	.0100
" to orbit .	.		. .	.0045
" of hind limb	.		. . .	.0070
" of hind foot .	.		. . .	.0170
Width of head behind .	.		. . .	.0060

This species belongs to the section called by Gray *Diplodactylus*. From Pacasmayo.

34. PHYLLODACTYLUS MICROPHYLLUS, sp. nov.

Small scales of the back and sides with larger ones scattered irregularly among them; these are not very much larger, not keeled, but smoothly convex, and a little smaller than the smooth, flat belly scales. Gular scales granular; labials to pupil $\frac{7}{7}$. Mental large, convex behind, bounded by four round scales of small size. Scales of top of muzzle twice as large as those of vertex. Tail scales uniform. Transverse scales of inferior side of the digits rather short; large plates of the end of the toes remarkably small, permitting the ungual phalange to project very freely. A row of prominent scales behind the thighs on each side of the base of the tail. Color very pale, with a few very indistinct transverse shades; in the young these shades are cross-bars.

				M.
Total length	.	.	. .	.101
Length to vent .	.		. .	.048
" to axilla	.	.	. .	.022
" to ear . .	.	.	. .	.012
" to eye . .	.	.	. .	.005
Width of the head behind	.		. .	.010
Length of hind limb	.		. .	.020
" of hind foot .			. .	.008

From the valley of Jequetepeque, Peru.

This species is intermediate between the last described, *P. inæqualis*, and such species as the *P. reissii* in the character of the squamation. In the small size of its distal laminæ of the digits, it differs from all the other species, and approaches the Australian genus *Stenodactylopsis* of Steindachner.

35. PHYLLODACTYLUS REISSII, Peters, Monatsber. Berlin Academy, 1862, p. 626.

From the valley of Jequetepeque.

36. THECADACTYLUS RAPICAUDA, Houttyn.

37. GONIODACTYLUS.

AMPHISBÆNIA.

38. AMPHISBÆNA OCCIDENTALIS, Cope, sp. nov.

Nasal, frontonasal, and parietal scuta in mutual contact in pairs, the last pair forming a half disk. Nasal not reaching lip; rostral protuberant, little visible from above, triangular in outline. Labials four above, three below; first superior longer than high, second higher than long, fourth very small. First labial twice as deep as long, second largest, longer than deep. Symphyseal narrowed and truncate behind, and bordered by a longitudinally oval plate, which also bounds the first and second labials below. A crescentic row of seven scuta bound the posterior borders of this and the labials, the median being the smallest. Ocular plate small, subquadrate, followed by four scales bordering each parietal to the median suture. Preanal scuta six, pores four, caudal annuli nineteen. Eye invisible.

Above, numerous scales dark-lead colored, interrupted by colorless ones. Below, white.

		M.
Total length		.285
Length to rictus oris		.006
" of tail		.023

Common in the valley of Jequetepeque. Allied to the *A. vermicularis* and *A. darwinii* of Duméril and Bibron. The former differs, among other points, in the possession of eight temporal scuta on each side; the latter has occipital scales, and only three superior labials.

39. AMPHISBÆNA FULIGINOSA, Linn.

OPHIDIA.

SCOLECOPHIDIA.

40. TYPHLOPS RETICULATUS, Linn.

From the Marañon.

TORTRICINA.

41. TORTRIX SCYTALE, Linn.

From the Marañon and Solimoens.

ASINEA.

42. EUNECTES MURINUS, L.
From the Amazon.

43. BOA CONSTRICTOR, L.
From the Solimoens.

44. XIPHOSOMA HORTULANUM, Lin.
From Iquitos on the upper Marañon.

45. LEPTOGNATHUS CATESBYI, Wieg.
From Rioja, Peru, the Marañon, Iquitos upper Marañon.

46. RHINOBOTHRYUM LENTIGINOSUM, Scopoli.

47. DIPSAS CENCHOA, L.
Iquitos.

48. SIBON ANNULATUM, L.
From the Solimoens.

49. GERRHOSTEUS PROSOPIS, Cope, Proceed. Acad. Philada. 1874, p. 71.
From Nauta, Peru.

50. SCYTALE CORONATUM, Linn.

51. OXYRRHOPUS FITZINGERII, Tschudi, Fauna Peruana Reptiles, p. 56.
Valley of Jequetepeque.

52. OXYRRHOPUS PETOLARIUS. Subsp. PETOLARIUS, L.

53. DRYOPHIS ARGENTEA, Daud.

54. LEPTOPHIS MARGINATUS, Cope; *Thrasops marginatus*, Cope, Proceed. Academy Philada.
1862, p. 349; *Ahætulla nigromarginata*, Günther, Ann. Magazine Nat. History, 1866.

55. LEPTOPHIS ORTONII, Cope, sp. nov.

Scales smooth, in fifteen series. Head rather short, muzzle equal or shorter than width between eyes. No loreal plate; postnasal about as large as prenasal plate; preoculars scarcely reaching frontal. Two postoculars. Temporals large, 1–2, followed by smaller scales. Superior labials nine, fifth, and sixth only bounding orbit. Seven lower labials in contact with geneials. Tail very long, two-fifths of the total. Gastrosteges not angulate, three times as wide as long.

	M.
Total length (No. 1) .	. .965
Length of tail (No. 1)	. .390
Total length (No. 2) .	. .950
Length of tail (No. 2)	. .400

45

Color above blue, a coppery golden spot within the apex of many of the scales, which extends on those of the external two rows, so as to cover the scale except at its base. Gastrosteges coppery-golden, the front margin sea-green. The blue scales have a black tip, and often a narrow border; the head is uniform green, except the yellow lips and a narrow black line along the upper margin of the posterior labials.

This splendid species is nearly allied to the *T. marginatus*, Cope, having the same short head and nasal scuta. It differs in its smooth scales, and in the coloration, for in that species the golden is entirely wanting, and the head scuta as well as the scales are broadly black bordered. The *T. marginatus* in addition has the gastrosteges strongly angulate and recurved on the sides, and only twice as wide as long.

Of my two specimens of *T. marginatus*, one has eight superior labials, as in the type, the other nine, on both sides. Their measurements are as follows:—

		M.
Total length (No. 1)	.	1.190
Length of tail (No. 2)	.	.460
Total length (No. 1)	.	1.155
Length of tail (No. 2)	. . .	.450

The *Leptophis ortonii* was discovered by Professor James Orton on the Solimoens or middle Amazon, and I take great pleasure in dedicating it to him as a token of esteem.

56. PHILODRYAS VIRIDISSIMUS, Linn.

From between Moyabamba and Balsa Puerto, Peru.

57. HERPETODRYAS HOLOCHLORUS, Cope, sp. nov.

Scales in ten longitudinal series, all wide, especially those of the first, which are as deep as long. The scales of the two vertebral rows are also wide, and all are smooth. The head is of normal form and size, with vertical lores, and eyes of moderate size. The rostral is as broad as high, the loreal a very little longer than high, and the preocular not reaching the frontal. Two postoculars, temporals 1–1; three scales only bordering the two parietals, whose posterior outline is strongly notched. The common suture of the parietals is shorter than the frontal and the superciliary. The frontal is narrowed behind, and the width in front less than the lateral sutures. Labials nine above, all rather low, fifth and sixth, and sometimes a corner of the fourth, entering the orbit; eleven inferior labials, of which seven are in contact with the geneials.

	M.
Total length (No. 1) .	.680
Length of tail (No. 1)	.220
Total length (No. 2) .	.685
Length of tail (No. 2)	.220

Anal plate entire in five specimens.

Color uniform green, pale on the lips and throat. In a young specimen (.340 m.) there are slightly black edged scales in small patches on each side of a pale vertebral band.

As compared with the *II. fuscus*, this species has a smaller eye at all ages, and a stouter form, including shorter tail. It bears the same relation to the form called *Dendrophis viridis*, by Duméril and Bibron.

From the Marañon. (No. 39.)

58. HERPETODRYAS CARINATUS, Linn.
From the lower Amazon.

59. HERPETODRYAS FUSCUS, Linn.
Two from Iquitos; one from the Solimoens, etc.

60. DRYMODIUS HEATHII, sp. nov.

Scales elongate, biporous, smooth, in seventeen longitudinal rows. Form slender, head narrow; the frontal shield with concave sides, much narrower behind than before, and one-fourth longer than the muzzle anterior to it. Parietals long. Postnasal higher and shorter than prenasal. Loreal long and low, lowest behind. One preocular not reaching frontal, two postoculars; temporals 2-2, long and narrow. Superior labials nine, fourth, fifth, and sixth, entering orbit; inferior labials ten, six in contact with genials. Pregenials only half as long as postgenials. Gastrosteges 188; anal divided; urosteges 116. Muzzle shorter than interorbital, width by nearly the diameter of the eye.

General color olivaceous-ashen; a broad, brown, dorsal band, which is darker edged, extends to the tail, involving five rows of scales. A brown band on each side involves the first, second, and third rows of scales, which are blackish tipped. Lips and below lighter, unspotted; a dark band from nostril through eye to last labial shield.

	M.
Total length	.780
Length of tail .	.240
" to rictus oris .	.019

This whip-snake is allied to the *Drymobius boddærtii*, especially to the pale-banded variety. It is a more slender species, with narrower head plates, especially the frontal and loreal.

Obtained in the valley of Jequetepeque, Peru, by Doctor Edwin R. Heath, to whom I take great pleasure in dedicating the species, as a testimony to his disinterested zeal in advancing natural history.

61. DRYMOBIUS BODDÆRTII, Seetz.

From the lower Amazon.

62. SPILOTES PICEUS, Cope, Proceedings Academy Philada. 1868, 105.

From the Marañon. Adult and young, the latter with narrow white cross-bands, as in the species of *Drymobius*.

63. SPILOTES PULLATUS, Linn.

64. XENODON COLUBRINUS, Gthr., Catalogue B. M. p. 55.

65. TACHYMENIS CHILENSIS, Schleg. Günther, Catal. p. 34.

From Lake Titicaca.

66. OPHEOMORPHUS MERREMMII, Wied.

67. LYGOPHIS PŒCILOSTOMUS, sp. nov.

Scales in nineteen rows, poreless; anal plate divided, dentition diacranterian. Frontal shield with concave sides, nearly as wide behind as before, twice as long as wide, its length one-half greater than that of the muzzle in front of it. Rostral little visible from above; postnasal higher than prenasal; loreal oblique, higher than long. Oculars 1–2, the preocular scarcely reaching frontal; temporals 1–2. Superior labials eight (nine on one side), fourth and fifth in orbit. Inferior labials nine, six in contact with genials. Postgenials the longer. Gastrosteges 206 ; urosteges 89.

Color above ashen-brown, with a series of short, dark, brown cross-bands, extending across seven or eight scales, and separated by two rows of scales. These break and alternate on the middle of the length, and then form a serrate band, which is on the tail a uniform longitudinal band. Lips and chin spotted with brown ; belly ashey.

Valley of Jequetepeque.

This snake is somewhat like the *Liophis chamissonis*, but belongs to another genus.

68. LIOPHIS REGINÆ, Linn.

69. LIOPHIS ALMADENSIS, Wagler.

From the Solimoens.

70. LIOPHIS TEMMINCKII, Schleg.; *Txniophis tantillus*, Girard.

71. LIOPHIS PYGMÆUS, Cope, Proceed. Academy Phila. 1868, p. 103.

72. TANTILLA CAPISTRATA, sp. nov.

Ocular plates 1–1; labials seven above, the seventh the largest, the third and fourth bounding the orbit. The postnasal smaller than the prenasal, well separated from the short preocular by the prefontal, which touches the second labial. Rostral not very prominent; frontal wide, much shorter than the large parietals. Temporals 1–1, long and narrow. First pair of inferior labials in contact, postgencials short. Scales of body in fifteen series. Gastrosteges 139; anal divided; urosteges 71.

All the scales above the second row are brown-bordered; below this row white. Head above black, except the muzzle, which is white to the line of the preocular plate; a large labial spot behind the eye, and the hinder border of the parietals. A black half collar connected with the black crown by a longitudinal bar.

Total length .136; of tail .035; to rictus oris .005.

Valley of Jequetepeque, Peru.

73. TANTILLA MELANOCEPHALA, Schl.

74. HELICOPS POLYLEPIS, Gthr., Ann. Magaz. Nat. Hist.

The Solimoens.

75. HELICOPS ANGULATUS, Linn.

From Iquitos on the Marañon.

76. RHABDOSOMA PŒPPIGII, Jan. Arch., p. Zoologia Modena II. 1862, 11.

77. RHABDOSOMA BADIUM, Dum. Bibr.

From the Solimoens. Several color varieties.

PROTEROGLYPHA.

78. ELAPS NARDUCCII, Jan.

79. ELAPS IMPERATOR, Cope, Proceed. Academy Philada. 1868, p. 110.

A strongly marked subspecies, characterized by the continuation of the black rings entirely round the body, and of the black color which replaces the red rings to the gastrosteges. Also by the almost entire black color of the head, and the dusky shade of the lighter parts of the lower surfaces.

From the Solimoens.

46

80. ELAPS CIRCINALIS, Dum. Bibron.

Four specimens from the valley of Jequetepeque. Of these, one has thirty-one black rings on the body; two have twenty-nine, and one has twenty-eight. All have the head black as far as the end of the parietals; the temporal scuta being included in the yellow neck band. Of five specimens from Eastern Costa Rica brought by Mr. Gabb, two have a similar coloration of the head, and in three the yellow collar crosses the occipitals. One has twenty-two black rings on the body, two have thirteen, and two eleven.

81. ELAPS TSCHUDII, Jan. Revue et Magazine de Zoologie 1859; Prodrome d'un Iconographie, etc., p. 13.

Numerous specimens from the valley of Jequetepeque are very constant in coloration. One of the most beautiful *Elapes*.

82. ELAPS ISOZONUS, Cope, Proceed. Academy Philada. 1860, p. 73-4.

83. ELAPS LEMNISCATUS, Linn.
Iquitos on the Marañon.

84. ELAPS SURINAMENSIS, Cuv.
The scales of the red intervals tipped with black. Two specimens from Iquitos on the Marañon.

SOLENOGLYPHA.

85. BOTHROPS BRASILIENSIS, Latreille.
The Marañon near the mouth of the Napo.

86. BOTHROPS MICROPHTHALMUS, Cope, sp. nov.

The maxillary fossette bounded in front by small scales, and below by two narrow scales. The superior labials number seven, of which the first two are small, and the third the largest, equalling the sixth; the fourth and fifth are shorter, and as high as long. The seventh is as long as the sixth, but lower. The fourth labial immediately under the pupil of the eye, and separated from it by two scales. Large and slightly keeled scales bound the labials above behind the eye. Nasals distinct, each higher than long, separated from the eye by a long preocular and a smaller loreal. Rostral plate rectangular, one-fourth higher than wide at the middle. Muzzle short, canthus rostralis bordered above by two scuta, and a scale next the superciliary plate, the scuta remarkably wide, the posterior pair separated by three large smooth scales on the summit of the muzzle. Superciliary shields three-fifths as wide as long, separated at the middle by two smooth scuta;

behind by five wide smooth scales. Scales of the top of the head smaller, sub-hexagonal, and smooth. Inferior labials ten, all wider than long. Scales of the body not elongate, in twenty-three longitudinal rows, the lower one or two rows smooth, the remainder keeled, but differently from what is observed in other species. Thus the keels do not reach the extremity of the scale, but terminate in an enlargement, which, on the posterior parts of the body, is a prominent tubercle. Gastrosteges 159; anal entire; urosteges 52.

Color above yellowish-brown, anteriorly uniform, and marked on the posterior two-thirds of the body with brown triangles on the sides, whose apices meet or approach on the middle line above. The interior at the base of the triangle is occupied by the ground color, which increases in extent anteriorly, so as to reduce the triangles to skeletons, and then obliterate them. Posteriorly the united triangles form cross-bands, which become united lengthwise on the tail, and finally confluent so as to form a uniform black. Head yellowish-brown above, yellow below, a yellow band extending from the eye to the side of the neck, which is bounded all the way by a brown band below. Belly yellow anteriorly, shaded increasingly with black to the end of the tail, a dark brown spot on the end of every second gastrostege on each side.

			M.
Length	.	.	.885
Length of tail	.	.	.125
" of rictus oris	.		.038
" to eye	.	.	.013
Width between eyes	.	.	.017
Diameter of eye (greatest)	.	.	.005

From between Balsa Puerto and Moyabamba, Peru.

This pit-viper is evidently a dangerous species, judging from the large size of its venom glands and length of its fangs. Associated with the development of the former, is the very small size of the eye, which is almost closed by the protuberant cheeks. The species is allied to the *B. diporus*, Cope, and *B. neuvidii*, Wagl. It differs, among other respects, in the smooth scales of the vertex, large in front and small behind.

ART. VIII.—*Note on the Ichthyology of Lake Titicaca.*

By E. D. COPE.

THE waters of the elevated plateaus of the Andes have been found to be the habitat of several peculiar genera of fishes, mostly belonging to the *Siluridæ* and the *Cyprinodontidæ.* Of the latter family two genera are now known, *Protistius*,[*] Cope, with one species from the Peruvian Andes, and *Orestias* (Cuvier and Valenciennes), of which six species have been described from the Lake Titicaca in the Bolivian plateau. Prof. James Orton, in his recent exploration of that region, procured specimens of four species of this genus from the Lake. On examination of these I find, unexpectedly to myself, that three of the species are new to science, and accordingly append descriptions of them. They are all in fine condition, and apparently adult.

1. ORESTIAS PENTLANDII, Cuv. Val., Vol. XVIII, p. 221.

2. ORESTIAS BAIRDII, Cope, sp. nov.

Established on a specimen eight and three-quarter inches long. Radii P. 17; D. 12; A. 16. Scales of the lateral line, counting from the line of the preoperculum, fifty. Scales larger above the operculum and rugose in that region, elsewhere smooth. Operculum about half covered with rugose scales; the lower limb of the preoperculum half as long again as the posterior, the scales small, rugose, and extending its entire length, leaving a naked band below the orbit. A few small, rough scales on the preorbital bone. Preorbital bone subquadrate, as long as high. Mouth directed vertically upwards. Top of the head entirely naked. A band of large rugose scales on the nape, with a naked space on each side of it.

The diameter of the eye is equal to the length of the muzzle, and enters the side of the head five times. The outline of the back and head is continuous and horizontal, the front flat, and over twice the long diameter of the eye. The head enters the length, minus the caudal fin, four and a quarter times, and the depth enters the same four and a half times. The depth of the head enters its length $1\frac{4}{5}$ times. The dorsal fin is further from the anal than the length of its base, and the margin of the caudal fin is openly concave.

This species is evidently nearest to the *O. cuvieri* of Valenciennes; it has a

---

* Proceedings Academy Philada. 1874, p. 66.

more elongated body and shorter fin bases. The head, according to Günther, is one-third the length in that fish, and the radii are A. 14–16; D. 18–19. It is dedicated to Professor Spencer F. Baird, the assistant secretary of the Smithsonian Institution, the *alma mater* of many naturalists of the present and coming generations.

3. ORESTIAS ORTONII, Cope, sp. nov.

Radii of the fins, P. 18; D. 16; A. 16. Dorsal outline gently arched to interorbital region, muzzle horizontal, narrowed, the mouth directed vertically upwards. Length of head one-fourth the total, minus the caudal fin, the greatest depth entering the same three and one-third times. Eye four and a half times in the length of the head, and twice in the interorbital width. Lower limb of preopercle three-fourths as long as the posterior. Scales of lateral line, beginning above anterior part of operculum, thirty-two. On the anterior part of the body they are thickened and enlarged, there being but eight rows from the base of superior ray of pectoral fin to the median nuchal row. They extend forwards to between the eyes, and cover the entire operculum, preoperculum, and suborbital bones. All are entirely smooth. The dorsal fin is further from the caudal than the length of its base. Preorbital bone deeper than long.

		M.
Total length		.162
Length to basis caudal fin		.133
" to basis anal fin		.082
" to operculum		.033
" to preoperculum		.022
" to orbit		.008
Depth of head at orbit		.026

Color silvery, the enlarged scales of the anterior part of the body green; head above black, sides yellow.

This species appears to be most nearly allied to the *Orestias owenii*, Cuv. Val., in the proportions of the head to the body, but the head is of a different form. Günther states that the head of *O. owenii* is "nearly three-fourths as long as high;" in *O. ortonii* it is two-thirds as high as long. The caudal peduncle is longer in *O. ortonii*, and the fin-rays of *O. owenii* are stated to be D. 14–5; A. 13–6. In *O. jussiæi* the body is shorter by one length of the head, and the radii are D. 14; A. 15.

This species is dedicated to Professor James Orton, of Vassar College, the indefatigable explorer of the Peruvian Andes.

4. ORESTIAS FRONTOSUS, Cope, sp. nov.

Fin radii D. 14–15 ; A. 15. Scales of lateral line (commencing above preoperculum), thirty-six. Dorsal region little arched, frontal region protuberant and convex in both longitudinal and transverse section, the profile then descending steeply to the upper lip. Mouth nearly vertical, eye four times in length of head of specimens eight inches long. The depth of the head at the posterior border of the orbits is exactly equal to the length, and its length is contained in the total (without caudal fin), four times in one, and three and three-quarter times in another specimen. The preorbital bone is higher than long, and the inferior border of the preoperculum is two-thirds the length of the posterior. Large, thickened, and smooth scales cover the anterior part of the body, and the operculum, preoperculum, and suborbital bones, and advance on the front to between the orbits. The depth of the body enters the length three and one-third times. Tail even or slightly convex.

				M.
Total length	. . .	.	.	. 0.190
Length to basis of anal fin		.	.	. .103
" of head .	.	.	.	. .038
" to orbit .	.	.	.	. .010
Interorbital width (axial)	.	. .	.	. .016

This *Orestias* is generally black, the belly having a pale yellowish color.

Its affinities are to the *O. ortonii*, but the difference in the form of the head is very striking. Dr. Günther describes the head of the *O. owenii* as deeper than long, and the posterior border of the preoperculum as equal to the lower, characters not possessed by the *O. frontosus.*

Two specimens were obtained by Prof. Orton, who states that they are called by the inhabitants "Caracha," while the *O. bairdii* and *O. pentlandii* are known as "Boga," and adds that all are excellent table fishes.

EXPLANATION OF PLATES.

PLATE I.

Batrachia, natural size.

Fig. 1. *Cranopsis fastidiosus;* 1a, mouth.
   2. *Crepidius epioticus;* 2a, mouth.
   3. *Ollotis cœrulescens;* 3a, mouth.
   4. *Bufo auritus.*
   5. *Bufo coccifer.*
   6. *Dendrobates talamancæ.*
   7. *Hyla nigripes.*
   8. *Phyllobates hylæformis;* 8a, mouth.
   9. *Lithodytes podiciferus.*
  10. *Lithodytes melanostictus;* 10a, mouth.
  11. *Lithodytes megacephalus;* 11a, mouth.
  12. *Trypheropsis chrysoprasinus;* 12a, mouth.

PLATE II.

Fig. 1. *Anolis insignis.*
   2.   "   *microtus.*
   3.   "   *pachypus.*
   4.   "   *oxylophus.*
   5. *Chalcidolepis metallicus.*

PLATE III.

Fig. 1. *Basiliscus plumifrons,* natural size; 1a, head from above.
   2. *Basiliscus mitratus;* head from above, natural size.

PLATE IV.

Fig. 1. *Dendrophidium melanotropis.*
   2. *Dryophis brevirostris.*
   3. *Hyla elæochroa;* 3a, mouth.
   4. *Hylodes cerasinus;* 3a, mouth.

PLATE V.

Fig. 1. *Leptognathus argus;* natural size.
   2. *Telcuraspis schlegelii;* natural size.
   3. *Bothriopsis proboscideus;* natural size.
   4. *Hyla uranochroa;* natural size.

PLATE VI.

Heads of *Lacertilia* and *Ophidia,* natural size.

Fig. 1. *Mabuia alliacea,* from above.
   2. *Chalcidolepis metallicus; a,* above; *b,* below.
   3. *Amiva gabbiana; a,* above; *b,* below.
   4. *Anolis trochilus,* above.
   5. *Anolis oxylophus,* above.
   6. *Xiphosoma annulatum;* in this and the following figures, the superior view is marked *a.* the lateral *b.*
   7. *Leptognathus argus* (*a*).
   8. *Leptognathus pictiventris* (*a* and *b*).
   9. *Leptophis æruginosus* (*a* and *b*).
  10. *Leptophis saturatus* (*a* and *b*).
  11. *Spilotes chrysobronchus* (*a* and *b*).
  12. *Contia calligaster* (*a* and *b*).
  13. *Bothriopsis proboscideus* (*a*).

Published Nov. 26, 1875.